How to Win Millions
Playing Slot Machines!

. . . or Lose Trying

A Scoblete
Get-the-Edge Guide

How to Win Millions
Playing Slot Machines!

. . . or Lose Trying

Frank Legato

Foreword by Frank Scoblete

Chicago and Los Angeles

Illustrations by Alexander Holzach

Cover design by Ken Toyama

Legato, Frank, 1956–
     How to win millions playing slot machines— or lose trying / Frank Legato ; foreword by Frank Scoblete.
          p. cm. — (A Scoblete get-the-edge guide)
     Includes index.
     ISBN 1-56625-216-4
     1. Slot machines. 2. Gambling. I. Title. II. Series.

GV1311.S56L44 2004
795.27—dc22
                                        2004003585

Bonus Books
875 North Michigan Ave., Ste. 1416
Chicago, IL 60611

Printed in the United States of America

For Karla

Table of Contents

Foreword by Frank Scoblete   xi

Introduction: Who the Hell Am I, Anyway?   xv

1   What Is a Slot Machine, Anyway?   **1**
Origins of the slot

2   I Know a Good Idea When I Steal It   **5**
*The history of the slot, from the mechanical game of the early
1900s to the invention of the computerized "virtual-reel" system*

3   Are There Gnomes Inside?   **11**
*What a modern slot machine is, what a modern slot machine is
not, and why you cannot control whether you win or lose*

4   Frequently High-Hitting Payback Percentage   **19**
*How to know what kind of game you're playing before you sit
down, and the difference between payback percentage and hit
frequency*

5   Yes, You Can Win   **25**
*No, I won't guarantee that you can win. But here are some tips
to reduce your chances of losing in the end, and your best chance
to walk away a winner*

6   You Can't Be Serious   **33**
*A look at the more preposterous myths that abound concerning
slot play, and why they are all nonsense*

7   But I've Got a System   **47**
*A look at some of the crazier "systems" for winning at slots that
can be found at your local bookstore, and why they're all scams*

8   **Join the Club**   55
     A look at slot clubs, how they were formed, why you should join,
     and all those damn key chains

9   **Is That Popeye or Mammy Yokem?**   63
     How slot manufacturers use branded themes and funny cartoons
     to suck your wallet dry

10   **Theme This**   71
     Some slot machine themes we'd like to see—and some comedy
     themes I came up with in columns that are now actual slot
     machines

11   **Who Was That Jerk? Oh, It Was Me**   77
     A look at slot machine behavior and etiquette, and some stories
     from the front lines about people who just don't get it

12   **Tales from the Road: Vegas**   85
     A look at the Mother of All Slot Towns

13   **Tales from the Road: Atlantic City**   105
     A look at slots in Atlantic City, "Where Life Begins at 90"

14   **Tales from the Road: The South**   117
     Biloxi, Tunica, New Orleans, and other slot spots where people
     are always "fixin'" to do things

15   **Tales from the Road: The North**   125
     Yes, there are slots in Detroit. And in Canada. And West Virginia
     and Delaware. Don't forget your fanny pack and long johns

16   **Tales from the Road: The Midwest**   131
     Slots amid the cornfields

17   **Tales from the Road: Racinos**   135
     The new rage in racetrack slots proves that, regardless of how
     lame a facility is, if you build slots, they will come

18   **The Modern Slot Jockey**   143
     A look at the characteristics of the people playing slots these days

19 It's Cool Being a Slot Expert   151
Some of the stuff I have enjoyed about my years covering the slots

Acknowledgments   157
Index   159

Foreword

by Frank Scoblete

I am so happy that Frank Legato has written a book, because what the world needs now, in this time of war, rumors of wars, disease, and strife, in this time of terrorism and emotional and economic upheaval, in this time of travail, is a sensitive, insightful, courageous, and honest journey into what it means to be a human being in a new and dangerous century. Unfortunately, Frank hasn't written about that; he's written a book about slot machines.

You might be wondering, just who is Frank Legato? And what makes his book so special compared to the other eight thousand books about slot machines that lie in the moldy corners of huge warehouses gathering dust and being discolored by rat turds?

To discover the truth about a person, who better to go to than his very own loving family? So I asked Frank's mother about him: "Frank? Don't know of any Frank." His children: "Daddy? You've *met* my daddy?" His wife: "Ugh."

Frank Legato has done many amazing things in his life, most of which can't be written about without getting him arrested. He is a card-carrying liberal, on the cutting edge of contemporary concerns. "I absolutely believe that most women should have the right to vote," says Frank.

He has been an advisor to presidents and heads of state. President Clinton often sought out Frank's advice when involved in sticky situations. A clever wordsmith, Frank helped Clinton out by giving him just the right things to say, such as "I didn't inhale," and "I did not have sex with that woman," and "It depends on what the meaning of is is."

Frank has worked his whole life in the peace movement and, according to him, "All throughout college I wanted a piece but I never got it."

Frank is a man of the people, who delights in making friendships. His two friends agree. "Frank is the kind of guy that, like, if you saw he was dying in the middle of the street or something, you'd really feel bad if a car ran over him," said friend Barney.

"Yeah," said his other friend, Dwayne.

Over the years Frank has held many important positions in the writing world. I tried to get in touch with his former employers, but there were so many of them, and none of them were able to return my calls when I left messages that I wanted to talk to them about Frank Legato. One former employer did answer a letter I sent him, but when I opened this person's envelope it exploded, so I wasn't able to find out all the good things this guy had to say about Frank.

Many of you reading this book have no idea as to the impact that Frank Legato's life and works have had on popular culture. Did you know that he has been the inspiration behind some of the best television commercials ever conceived? Frank so inspired his wife on their honeymoon that she went on to write two of the most revered commercials of all time, "Where's the beef?" and "I've fallen and I can't get up."

You would think that with all of this success Frank would be an arrogant, pompous, self-aggrandizing, self-centered, bulbous windbag. And so what if he is?

When you read this book you'll see why, too.

Frank has a foolproof method for beating the slot machines, which he reveals on page . . . on second thought, maybe you should buy this book and not try to find out the secret without paying for it. But that's not all this book is about. It's not just about winning millions and millions playing the slots, guaranteed. . . . Oh, yeah— Frank says that if you don't win at least, *at least,* a million dollars using his methods of play then he will, *Frank* will, *that* Frank . . . *Legato* . . . not *this* Frank writing *this* foreword . . . *Scoblete* . . . that *Frank Legato,* known as the man *himself* to his probation officer, will pay you a million dollars out of his own pocket, even if it means that his great-grandchildren starve to death on the streets of Beverly Hills. If, after one century of playing the slots the way Frank Legato says you should, you have not amassed a million dollars, then you can get that million by writing to Frank Legato in care of whatever cemetery or urn he's in. Frank promises to make a supernatural effort to see to it that you get that million. He also promises to find out if Houdini still exists.

But that's not all you get when you read this book. No, sir.

What this book offers you is a fun-filled journey into the mind of someone who is, quite literally, out of his mind—driven there by those infernal slot machines that *you* want to play. By journeying into his mind, you get to occupy all that empty space, see. And isn't that what everyone wants, plenty of space?

And you'll also learn so much about the slot machines that you'll be able to wow people at your next church or temple service with stories about your gambling habit, uh, hobby. Now, won't that be impressive to the priest or minister or rabbi and the congregation? Sure will.

And don't be one of these wiseacres who think that there is nothing to know about slot machines. That you just put your money in and hope you win. Would Frank have written a whole book about slot machines if there weren't a whole book's worth of knowledge about these machines? No. You think he just did it to make money? No. Do you think the sanitarium will release Frank soon? No.

But just think on this: When you finish reading this book, you too will be able to hold your head up high and say with all the rest of us when discussing the author of this book, "Frank who?"

So learn and, most important, enjoy! Because, kidding aside, there is a wealth of information in this book!

Introduction

Who the Hell Am I, Anyway?

I was born in the house my father built.

No, wait. That was Nixon.

I was born in a hospital in Pittsburgh, Pennsylvania. The year was 1956. Nixon was vice president then, and probably didn't even realize that I was being born, which shows you what he knew of important world events. My parents, meanwhile, took one look at me and knew that I was going to grow up to be an expert on slot machines.

Seriously, though, no one really knew I was going to be an expert on slot machines. It wasn't something I told the kindergarten teacher in 1961 when she asked all the children what they wanted to be when they grew up. ("Timmy wants to be a fireman. Frankie, what do you want to be?" "I wanna be an experp on slop machines.") When I was a kid, all I really wanted to be was a Beatle. (I'm still waiting to hear from Ringo and Sir Paul.)

The real reason I became an "experp on slop machines" is a long story. But hey, this is a book.

The reason I became a slot expert was, in fact, Nixon. I entered college in 1974, a few weeks after Nixon resigned the presidency because he'd had his political pants pulled down by journalists Carl Bernstein and Bob Woodward. By 1976, I, like my fellow students, was told I would have to declare a major. After we all came to grips with the fact that no one was going to give us a job that involved smoking massive amounts of marijuana for 40 hours a week, every one of us who was in college in 1976 declared *journalism* as his or her major, because we had all just seen *All the President's Men* after smoking massive amounts of marijuana.

Consequently, when we all graduated in 1978 with journalism degrees, there were no writing jobs available for most of us—at least those of us in Pittsburgh. Now, at that moment in history, Pittsburgh was still synonymous with traditional smokestack industry. Big industries were still spewing industrial pollutants into the air of Western Pennsylvania at an alarming rate, which to us was a good thing; smoke meant employment. The city motto was "Don't Trust Air You Can't See."

Every Western Pennsylvanian in college during the 1970s had parents in one of the main industries—steel, coal, glass, electrical engineering, railroads, banking, or ketchup. In Pittsburgh, a college graduate who couldn't find a job in his or her chosen field went into whatever the family industry was. For my family, that was railroads. My parents met on the railroad. On my mother's side, my grandfather and great-grandfather were railroaders. I had the rails in my blood. So, obviously, I had to become a slot expert.

No, I had to work for the railroad. I became a clerk for Conrail, which was short for Consolidated Amalgamated Agitated Railified Railroad Incorporated, Limited. My railroad career lasted three years, by which time Nixon had passed my fate on to Gerald Ford, who had given it to Jimmy Carter, who had handed it off to Ronald Reagan.

President "Dutch" Reagan initiated a plan called "trickle-down economics." Under this economic theory, extreme wealth is granted to a few people who are already rich. That wealth "trickles down" until every blue-collar job in the nation is eliminated and the middle class is wiped out entirely. Thus, I was laid off from the railroad.

After a couple years of freelance writing (definition: "writing performed by the unemployed"), and after going to graduate school with a major in public affairs (definition: "reporter who couldn't find a job"), I went to Washington, D.C., where lots of writing jobs were available. And lots of big buildings with statues. There, I found a job writing for and editing a magazine about big buildings with statues.

Actually, the job I found was writing for and editing a magazine covering the obvious subject of interest in our nation's capital: the casino industry. The magazine was called *Public Gaming*, and it was based in Rockville, Maryland—up the "Beltway" from Washington. (The Beltway is a highway famous for its historic perfection of bumper-to-bumper, 70-mile-per-hour driving.)

My first published article in *Public Gaming* concerned Aristocrat Leisure Industries, an Australian slot machine manufacturer trying to become licensed to sell its games in Nevada. This article brought to light, for the first time, my astute knack for "reading the market," as I predicted, right then in August of 1984, that Aristocrat would indeed become licensed to sell its games in Nevada. Sure enough, they did become licensed—16 years later, in the year 2000. But, anyway, I was soon editor of a new magazine from the same publisher, called *Casino Gaming*. I started going to trade shows, where the very latest in slot machine technology was demonstrated by men in Elvis costumes.

After I left that company, I continued to write about slots for a number of different magazines. I ended up at Casino Journal Publishing Group, as "Slots Editor" for *Casino Journal*, a trade publication, and *Casino Player*, a regular, for-the-masses, read-on-the-john magazine. In 1998, we started a new magazine called *Strictly Slots*, which is, remarkably, strictly about slots. I served as editor of that for a while.

I still write for those player magazines, although I recently left my full-time job at *Strictly Slots* to help start up a new trade journal, *Global Gaming Business*. I am now senior editor of the new trade journal. I also juggle and perform various parlor tricks. (Available for bar mitzvahs, smokers, and birthday parties. Rates reasonable.)

All this adds up to me being a writer who has researched and written about a single subject, slot machines, for what amounts to a pathetically long period of time. Through sheer rote, I became an expert. I know more about the contraptions than anyone should ever want to know. I know their history, inner operations, how they work, how they hit, how they don't hit, and how often they go to the bathroom. Now people often place my cartoon-like face in front of television cameras to talk about slot machines.

So that's how I became an expert, and as you can now see it's all Nixon's fault.

There are other experts on slot machines, and I know as much about the subject as any of them. But as the Wizard of Oz told me during a recent delusional episode, "There is one thing they have that you don't have: a book." People have been telling me for years that I should write a book about slots. So that's what I'm doing. But since there are already more than a few good books out there about slot machines I wanted to come up with a new "angle." A "gimmick" that no one else has tried. A slot-machine *coup de grace* (literally, "French words in italics").

People always liked the goofy column I do in *Strictly Slots* called "Perfectly Frank." (Get it?) It is a humor column, sort of like a slot-machine Dave Barry. (In fact, before I ever read a word that Dave Barry wrote, people were telling me I write like Dave Barry. After reading a ton of Dave's stuff, I have determined that it is he who writes like me.)

So I've decided to combine my knowledge of slot machine history and operations with the oft-skewed vision of the world that I employ for "Perfectly Frank"—what I call on my business card "Eccentricity Bordering on Dementia." In this book, it is my intention to give you a complete course on the modern slot machine, with side orders of jocularity, tomfoolery, and haberdashery.

But, before you read another word, I must caution you: Anything in these pages that people conclude to be "funny" is probably a joke. Don't take it seriously. Don't become offended.

If you do take offense, well, I hope you paid for the book first.

Chapter 1

What Is a Slot Machine, Anyway?

Before we get into all the hard stuff about slots—which may or may not involve a "pop quiz" now and then to make sure you're paying attention ("Marvin, would you like to share that joke with the entire class?")—I thought I would start chapter 1 by attempting to cram as many words as I possibly could into a single sentence.

That accomplished, I'd like to define exactly what it is we're talking about. What is this thing we refer to as a "slot machine?"

Webster's "Collegiate" Dictionary, which comes equipped with holders for beer cans, defines the term "slot machine" thusly: "a machine operated by inserting a coin in its slot, esp. a gambling device or a vending machine." We'll concentrate on the type of machine rumored to be a "gambling device." I will cover the other kind of machine in my upcoming book *Gumball Machines: The Naked Truth*.

Actually, the term "slot machine" was created to describe a gambling device. Back in 1803, frontiersman Jeremiah Slot carved the first wooden "Slot's Machine" out of a block of wood from a felled oak tree. He pulled a branch on the side of the block and acorns came falling out. Soon, he set up shop and charged his fellow pioneers a nickel a pop to "go for the acorns." In return, he gave each customer a key chain.

Seriously, though, "slot machine" is actually short for "nickel-in-the-slot machine." These were games of chance located in bars and on street corners around San Francisco at the dawn of the 20th century. (At night, too.) It was another one of those "wacky California things" back then: In the early 1890s, entrepreneurs "back East" had invented these big, ornate hunks of furniture with fancy roulette wheels imbedded in them. Unable to figure out what the hell they had just created, they sent them to San Francisco. "Those nutty Californians will come up with something," they said to each other. The Californians saw that there was a crank to turn the wheel, and if the wheel landed on certain spots a bunch of acorns fell out. Always up for another "harebrained scheme," the Californians said, "Let's have people win money or prizes instead of acorns!" San Francisco saloonkeepers placed them in their watering holes, and slot machine gambling was born.

Barflies would put a nickel into the slot and turn the cranks on these things, and maybe win a free drink or cigar, or Wayne Newton tickets. There was a little group of German immigrants in San Francisco (okay, they weren't *that* little) that began improving on the big machines with other big machines. But they were all too big—they were about the size of jukeboxes. Since no one had invented records yet, the Germans began working on smaller machines. Some were poker machines that fit right on the bar, with five little spindles, each holding teeny cards. For a nickel, the cards would spin like bitty Rolodexes until they stopped on a five-card poker hand.

You wouldn't find expert gamblers like Bob Dancer, John Robison, or Skip Hughes playing these poker machines, though. Why? Because they weren't born yet. But, even if these fellows were to somehow find themselves in a dusty San Francisco saloon of the 1890s, surrounded by sweaty Germans and smoke from stinking cheroots, they wouldn't play these poker games. You see, the machines used a single deck of cards spread evenly across the five spindles. Now, God knows I'm no mathematical genius, but it seems to me the 52 cards of a normal deck would not spread evenly over five spindles. The inventors of the games realized this too. But rather than getting their knickers in a twist over the problem they just left two cards out. Much like myself, they were operating two cards short of a full deck.

The cards they left out were invariably high cards of different suits, so the odds of landing a royal flush were cut in half. The odds of getting four of a kind or any number of high straights were cut too. Probably a lot. (Someone should figure that out.) Finally—as if all that weren't bad enough—the saloons actually offered no cash back.

Consequently, the odds of "hitting the big one" on the poker machines were equivalent to the odds of a horse walking into the bar and ordering a sarsaparilla. (Bonus joke: Horse walks into a bar. Bartender says, "Why the long face?") It didn't really matter all that much, though, because these poker games awarded drinks or cigars as the prizes. The ones that awarded drinks were popular with bar owners, because if someone won the one-hundred-drink top prize it was a pretty good bet the guy would be unconscious before he finished collecting. The next day, he would wake up and have no idea whether he'd finished collecting, or even what he had been trying to collect, or why he had slept in a drainage ditch that night.

On other poker machines, a royal flush won you, like, a hundred cigars. This pretty much guaranteed that the main venues for these poker games would be cigar stores. Eventually, our group of German San Francisco inventors from four paragraphs back noticed that some people were becoming tired of going into the cigar store with two sacks of nickels and coming out smoking a 10-cent cigar that had cost them two hundred dollars. They started inventing machines that dispensed real coins as the prizes. Cash. Filthy lucre. Coin of the realm. Sometimes called "jack." The newly invented gambling devices would award players with a "pot" full of "jack." Thus was born that now-common nickname for slot prizes, "reportable win."

Remarkably, many people preferred winning money to winning a cigar. (Besides, the cigars caused a real mess in the counting machine at coin redemption.) The money-paying games would cause the first "revolution" in the design of a slot machine.

Two German San Francisco inventors achieved particularly notable success. Gustav Schultze invented wheel machines with automatic pay mechanisms that spilled coins to the delight of patrons. (He would go on to play a German sergeant on *Hogan's Heroes*.)

But Charles August Fey built the most significant new contraption in 1899. It had three spring-loaded, spinning reels, each bearing pictures of bells, horseshoes, stars, or card suits. There was a handle on the side that it took a team of oxen to pull. But when that was accomplished the reels would spin around until stopped by a separate mechanism. Most of the time, that was that. For a nickel, the customer had experienced several seconds of unimaginable bliss from watching spinning reels. But, once in a while, the reel symbols matched up, and a "pot" of "jack" would fall out. Customers went berserk:

CUSTOMER: I'm rich! Why, there must be $2 worth of nickels in that pile!
CUSTOMER'S WIFE: But, Durwood, you put at least $15 worth of nickels into the slot.
CUSTOMER: Who cares? Look at that pile of nickels!

After witnessing this, the saloonkeepers knew that there were millions of Durwoods out there just dying to empty the nickels out of their pockets.

Things would never be the same.

Chapter 2

I Know a Good Idea When I Steal It

Charles August Fey called his new three-reel contraption the Liberty Bell, because it was a trend among slot machine manufacturers around 1899 to give stuff patriotic names. Also, it was a big improvement over his wife's suggestion, the "Bet Five Nickels to Win Two Nickels Game."

Although Charlie Fey didn't know it at the time, his three-reel design was to be the model on which all future slots would be based. The basic mechanics and design of that machine would be emulated by slot machine inventors around the country.

By "emulated," I mean "stolen." Two years before Fey revealed his revolutionary machine, a judge had declared that the U.S. patent laws did not apply to slot machines because the things had no "utility"—no useful purpose, other than separating people from their money. That would eventually be changed, of course, when separating people from their money became a useful purpose for an invention. (I think the law was changed so they could patent the "Chia Pet.")

Anyway, Fey tried to protect his invention by refusing to sell or lease a Liberty Bell machine to anyone. He would keep his machines and use them only at venues he owned or licensed. To copy it, someone would have to steal one of his machines.

Guess what happened?

It took six years, but in 1905 someone stole a Liberty Bell from a San Francisco saloon. (Witnesses said the thief was a one-armed bandit.) It turned up in Chicago, where in 1906, by sheer coincidence, Herbert Mills introduced the Mills Liberty Bell. Within a few years, there was also a Caille Liberty Bell in Detroit, another Liberty Bell in Chicago manufactured by Fey's lifelong friend Tom Watling (who, incidentally, looked exactly like Mr. Monopoly), and Liberty Bells of all kinds from all manufacturers, including My First Liberty Bell (Fisher-Price).

But the Mills Liberty Bell would meet with particular success across the country, because Herbert Mills was the first manufacturer to apply mass-marketing and assembly-line manufacturing principles to slot machine production. He was known as the Henry Ford of Slot Machines. (This was back when the real Henry Ford was still known as the Herbert Mills of Automobiles.)

In any event, by 1909 three-reel slot machines were all over the place. But, that very year, those darned "goody two-shoes" got into the game—you know, those people who say gambling is "bad." Slot machines were outlawed in San Francisco, then in the rest of California, and even in Nevada.

But this was not necessarily a bad thing for the early slot-makers. They just made the things into gum dispensers. Every nickel you put in would get you a pack of gum from a dispenser on the side, and if the reel symbols matched you got, like, a thousand packs of gum.

No, not really. You got tokens for merchandise, or for free plays on the gum machine. With a wink and a nudge, some saloon owners would give you money for lining up jackpot combinations.

The fact that slots were, well, kind of illegal did little to hurt business. What it did to was to create new symbols for the reels—fruit symbols, to represent fruit gum, and "bar" symbols, which looked like the bars on the gum packages. It also let slot machine owners placed them out in public as "gum venders," in spots where even little kids could play them.

All that changed in 1919, when Prohibition took the booze out of the saloons and sent it underground through the creation of the speakeasy. Good citizens would no longer be subjected to the evils of gambling devices disguised as gum machines. Now they could go into a speakeasy and play a slot machine that made no bones about being a gambling device. The slot business took off like never before. By the time the Great Depression hit, the three-reel contraptions were at the height of their early popularity—just in time for Nevada to legalize gambling in 1931.

Slots were again "legit," at least in one state that at the time contained about three residents, two prairie dogs, and an iguana. In the rest of the country, they were still popular, as long as the sufficient number of official palms were greased. Periodically, mayors of big cities would get pictures taken swinging a sledgehammer at confiscated "illegal" slots, but, other than that, slots were in all the big Northern cities.

(But, still, no cash back.)

Things went on like this through World War II, but things in Nevada really started hopping after the war. Bugsy Siegel took over the Flamingo and got rubbed out. The Rat Pack started their wacky shenanigans, and all the old slot manufacturers—Mills, Jennings, Pace, Watling, Shmatling, and on and on—sold games to Nevada casinos. By 1960, when Frank, Dean, Sammy, and the boys made *Oceans Eleven*, one-armed bandits were a Nevada staple. Everybody else, who generally had two arms, played slot machines.

Well, not really. Back then, slots were still generally played by the ladies—something to do while their husbands played at the tables. All that was about to change, though.

In the early '60s, slots still worked in basically the same way as the Fey Liberty Bell. No one had changed the basic design during the century. But right about then work was already under way that would provide, in 1964, a revolutionary change. It was all, of course, thanks to four lovable mop-tops from Liverpool, England, who—

No, wait. Wrong story.

The change in slot machines would come from Bally Manufacturing, a Chicago company that had first tried changing the basic design of slots in 1941 with a machine called the Club Bell, a "console" slot (basically, a wooden cocktail table that paid) that accepted multiple coins with jackpots that rose according to the wager. Within a year, the slot manufacturers would all retool for production of war materials, but after the war ended there was still one problem—Illinois had implemented a law that prohibited the manufacture of gambling devices. Bally became known for its pinball machines after that—until Illinois repealed the ban on making slots in 1963. Bally picked up where it had left off, and in 1964 introduced a slot machine called Money Honey.

Money Honey wasn't just mechanical. It was *"electro-mechanical."* It was all lit up. It made sounds that actually went beyond *ding*. It was "multicoin." It had lots of paying combinations. It danced around the floor and sang "Shortnin' Bread" in five languages.

Okay, I made the last one up. But one more thing Money Honey did have was a "hopper"—a large compartment that held lots of coins for jackpots, with a hopper tray, a big bowl into which coins made a loud "clang" as they dropped—as opposed to the old-style game, which basically spit coins from tubes into a dish. And this one dropped more coins than the old games—a "whopping" 84 or 85 percent of all coins wagered.

Within the ensuing five years, Bally came up with a bunch more innovations that made the jackpots larger—more reels, more coins in. There was the six-coin, four-reel Continental, with a "highboy" cabinet and a pay table that looked like the financial page of a newspaper. There was the five-reel Big Win, which had a top jackpot of (Gasp!) three thousand simoleons. Bally was smokin', and the other slot-makers were basically standing there watching, with their mouths open.

Players, meanwhile, started actually looking at slot machines as a real alternative to table games. But it was in the mid-1970s when casino owners, by that time wearing polyester suits with their black shirts and white ties, actually started looking at slot machines as a way to make money. That was thanks to another Bally innovation, a dollar-sized hopper. Dollar slot machines were put in carousels in Northern Nevada—high-payback games with lots of thousand-dollar-plus jackpots. Players went bonkers, and it began to dawn on casino owners that people would actually play slots with big jackpots. And, if they lost, they would play them some more. Casinos bought more and more Bally slots.

By the time Atlantic City swung open its doors in 1978, Bally controlled around 90 percent of the slot market. Meanwhile, Bally technicians and casino operators were putting their noggins together to come up with ways to offer even bigger jackpots. There were two ways to do this—more possibilities among the reel results, so the odds of winning big were longer; or requiring higher initial wagers. They couldn't fit more than five reels into a box unless they wanted two-game slot banks. They could raise the wager, though—and they did, creating $5 games, $25 games . . . all the way up to $100 games and $500 games.

They could also stretch the odds of winning a big jackpot by cramming more symbols and blanks—known as "stops"—onto each reel. Reels went from 22 stops to 25 stops. Then they stopped. The limits had been reached on what could physically be done to a game to offer higher jackpots without giving away the store. And, for the workhorse nickel and quarter games, those jackpots were still only a few hundred dollars. Something else would have to be done.

Hey, I know! Computers!

A computer programmer named Inge Telnaus worked with Bally during the late '70s on ways to make the jackpots bigger and still have slots make money. It dawned on Inge (known as "Inkie" to his friends) that if you could have reels that were, like, 10 feet long, each with hundreds or thousands of symbols, then you could offer zillion-dollar jackpots, which people would hardly ever hit, because the odds would be roughly equivalent to the odds of giant purple boll weevils attacking Las Vegas.

Telnaus got to work on an invention that was to revolutionize the slot industry. After much painstaking research, though, his wife told him he would have to get rid of all the 10-foot reel strips because she couldn't fit the car in the garage. So Telnaus figured out a way to make "imaginary" reel strips. Numbers would be plugged into a computer program to correspond to each symbol and blank on a regular-sized reel strip. Then more numbers would be assigned to the same symbols. Lots of numbers would be assigned to the blanks and low-paying symbols; only a few would be given to the high-paying symbols. A random number generator program would cycle through all the numbers and pick one—the odds were that it would be a low-paying number.

The effect would be the same as having a slot machine with reel strips extending to the stratosphere, except that no airplanes would be in danger of hitting them. Because they weren't actually reels. They were "virtual reels." Telnaus patented his invention under the snappy title "Electronic Device Utilizing a Random

Number Generator for Selecting the Reel Stop Positions." It would soon be known to everyone in the trade by the simple acronym "EDUARNGFSTRSP."

Overnight, it was possible to lose money at an alarming rate on a slot machine. Casino owners, just like the San Francisco saloon-keepers 80 years earlier, took note.

And, once again, things would never be the same.

Chapter 3

Are There Gnomes Inside?

The invention of EDUARNGFSTRSP is the sole distinguishing factor of the modern slot machine, and the sole reason Durwoods and Ralph Kramdens and countless other "regular Joes" began to give up their spots in lotto ticket lines to go play slots in casinos. Suddenly, the casinos could advertise big jackpots. I'm talking *big*. Burn-the-mortgage big. Tell-the-boss-to-cram-it big. Move-into-neighborhoods-full-of-people-you-used-to-hate-because-they-fell-ass-backward-into-money-even-though-they-are-total-pinheads big.

What was most appealing about these big payoffs was that, to win them, you didn't necessarily have to know anything about gambling. In fact, to win them, you didn't necessarily have to know anything about walking erect. Big casino gamblers had always been viewed either as suave, sophisticated types with money to burn, or as seasoned experts who knew the odds and strategy necessary to beat the house at its own game. Here was a casino game that could make someone rich, and could be successfully navigated by a drooling monkey with brain damage.

Telnaus received his patent for the virtual-reel system in 1984. A year or so later, in the slot-industry version of the sale of

Manhattan, he sold the rights to the invention. The company that bought the rights to this fancy new technology was a small Reno firm called International Game Technology. At the time, IGT (pronounced "Eye-Gee-Tee") mainly made video poker games and primitive video slots (played, of course, by primitive slot players). But, once armed with the Telnaus virtual-reel patent, IGT game developers went crazy. Then, after they were confined to various state institutions, they started creating reel-spinning slot games that have lasted to this day. IGT would soon rise to the top of the slot-manufacturing market.

But first the young company would introduce an unrelated, but no less revolutionary, idea. The first big robbery of players from lotto lines came in the mid-1980s. Engineers at IGT borrowed new-fangled "modem" technology from the world of office computers to link slot machines at casinos across Nevada to a single jackpot by using phone lines. A portion of each dollar placed in each machine would increment a giant, lottery-style, take-this-job-and-shove-it jackpot. Borrowing a title from Eastern lotteries, IGT called it "Megabucks." IGT introduced it in March of 1986 with a gala event hosted by Rich Little at the Stardust in Las Vegas.

(Incidentally, there was a 29-year-old reporter in the back of the room that day who had bloodshot eyes and was very close to vomiting, thanks to having been taken the night before on a drinking binge by a group of Australians from slot manufacturer Aristocrat. That was me. I had awakened that morning with sand in my pockets and no clue how I had arrived at my hotel. I have no idea what Rich Little said, or what IGT founder Si Redd said, or whether I even had matching shoes on my feet. Thank God for press kits. But I digress. . . .)

Megabucks transferred the phenomenon of "jackpot fever" from lotteries to casinos, as people fell over themselves to play the slots when the jackpots rose to the tens of millions of dollars. The first "Megabucks Millionaires" began to grin behind big checks in the pages of gaming magazines.

But, for the thousands of other players who did not happen to win the oversized checks, the recreational activity of pumping millions of coins into a slot, pulling a handle, and saying curse words would soon become a bit tiresome. No problem—the slot manufacturers were already in the process of making the games more interesting, thanks to the Telnaus patent. Within another five years, IGT, Bally, and a few other companies had issued a new generation of reel-spinners that paid large jackpots, dispensed bonuses for wild symbols, and drank Pepsi and rebelled against the older generation of slot machines. This was the period when games like IGT's Double Diamond, with its multiplying wild symbols, and Bally's Blazing 7s, with its blazing 7s, were created.

These games became incredibly popular, mainly because they had special features that resulted in players, on occasion, actually winning money. Double Diamond included a wild symbol that doubled your jackpot on any winning combination. If two of the wild symbols landed together with a paying symbol, the jackpot was quadrupled. This feature spawned a line of Double Diamond descendents from IGT, like Triple Diamond, Double Double Diamond, Double Triple Diamond, Double Triple Quadruple Quintuple Diamond Plus Five, and on and on, eventually to include Five Times Pay, Ten Times Pay, and Six-and-Seven-Eighths-Times Pay.

Other manufacturers, in the grand tradition of the early slot-makers, "emulated" this gimmick, producing slot games that were just like Double Diamond, only different: Double Jackpot Times Two. The Double Wild Symbol Game. Dubble Dye Mound.

The other popular style of game that allowed players to actually win money now and then loaded the pay schedule with winning combinations—so the player, instead of spending three hundred dollars with the hope of an occasional big jackpot, would dribble through those three C-notes while experiencing the "thrill" of lots and lots of smaller jackpots.

One way to accomplish this was to load the program up with "7" combinations. Slot players love the number "7." They get excited when they see it landing all over the place on the reels, even if they don't form a winning combination. If three of them line up together, it triggers a raucous celebration, even if the resulting payout is a quarter. The idea of including three or four winning "7" combinations in a game first came from an inventor at a slot manufacturer called Universal, but, after applying its own math and artwork to the concept, Bally came up with Blazing 7s, the most popular game in its history. Inevitably, other slot-makers "emulated" them: Flaming 7s. Lucky 7s. Sevens Flambeau. Sevens 'R' Us.

Another way to get lots of little hits was to load up the program with "dribble wins" from any combination of three symbols. IGT led this trend with Red, White, and Blue. Jackpot combinations would result from: three same-colored symbols; any red, white, and blue symbol in sequence; a single, double, and triple bar in sequence; three nonmatching pictures of former child stars who became drug addicts; and any number of other combinations. Players found interesting diversions not only in all the little 10-coin payouts, but also in staring at the encyclopedic pay schedule with stupid looks on their faces.

And, again, the copycat games followed: The Patriotic Color Game. Red, White, and Mauve.

These basic game programs were so effective that IGT and Bally are still creating spin-offs to this day. IGT uses Double Diamond and Red, White, and Blue as starting points for any number of bonus games—as does Bally with Blazing 7s. Of course, nowadays the classic reel-spinners constitute portions of slot floors that are populated with games that bear little resemblance to the traditional one-armed bandits. That's because of what happened in the late 1990s.

Beginning around 1996, manufacturers began combining reel-spinning slot machines with top boxes that included completely different games—known as "bonus games," or "games within games," or "games with additional ways to lose even more money."

It all started with the "wheel." A company called Anchor Games, which before the mid-'90s was mainly a slot route operator, came up with the idea of taking a roulette wheel and mounting it in the top of a slot box. An extra symbol on the reels would trigger a "bonus round" in which the player got the chance to spin the wheel for bonus money. Bally was the first to release a slot game incorporating the concept; the game was called Wheel of Gold.

But IGT would use the wheel to trigger yet another new trend—the use of a familiar entertainment brand to market a slot machine. The company already owned a license to use the popular TV game show *Wheel of Fortune* as a theme for a slot game, and had in fact used it to create an unsuccessful video slot. This time, they dressed up Anchor Games' wheel to look like the big fortune wheel used on the game show. The slot glass was decked out with artwork from the show, and a sound bite was blared through the slot speakers so that, when the extra reel symbol landed, the player heard the studio audience from the *Wheel* show chant, "WHEEL. OF. FORTUNE!"

Other than these slight modifications, and the fact that that the base game was Double Diamond instead of Blazing 7s, the *Wheel of Fortune* slot machine was no different from Bally's Wheel of Gold slot machine. But, as slot-makers were about to learn, Americans will automatically gravitate toward anything that even hints at being related in any way to television. You could put a box of weasel manure on a slot floor, and Americans would insert coins into it if it had a TV name. And it doesn't matter what TV name you give it. Call it the *MacNeil/Lehrer Report* Bonus, the Weather Channel Game, the Test Pattern Bonus . . . it doesn't matter. Americans will play it. *Wheel of Fortune* became one of the most successful slot machines in history.

But it was not just the TV theme that players liked. Surprisingly, players also liked machines that actually did something other than eating money and spinning reels around. Anchor Games started building slot machines with any number of unrelated games attached to the top. There was a slot with a pinball machine on top. There were slots with arcade games on top. There was even a slot with two other slots on top of it. Anchor became the Dr. Moreau of the slot machine industry. (The company was eventually bought by IGT, as were a couple other slot manufacturers, some computer system manufacturers and electronic display manufacturers, and several families from Iowa.)

These ideas would also be "emulated" by other slot manufacturers—but now patents were involved. Thus, an entirely new specialty developed in the legal profession; attorneys built entire careers in the field of Slot Theme Litigation.

But an entirely different style of gaming machine was gaining popularity at the same time Anchor was attaching kitchen sinks and transmissions from '42 Fords to slot machines. Remember Aristocrat? That was the Australian slot manufacturer that was the subject of my first-ever gaming article and the employer of those Australians who got me drunk in 1986. In the mid-'90s, Aristocrat introduced *video* slots in the Indian casinos and gaming riverboats that had been popular for years in Australia. Instead of a single "payline"—the line where the jackpot symbols land—these games had five paylines, or nine paylines, or more. A video screen displayed five animated reels, and the player would win money for matching up symbols horizontally, diagonally, verticaliy, in a pattern forming the shape of Lyle Lovett, and every other which way.

The effect was that the player would win something on almost every other spin. The machine would play funny tunes and congratulate the player for winning, even if he had inserted five coins to win two coins. (Sound familiar?) The games were awash in the "Durwood effect" I described in chapter 1—"Look at all those coins!" And that was just in the primary game. They also had something called a "second-screen bonus game," which had the same effect as the mechanical bonus games that were plunked on top of the reel-spinning slots. The animated reels would disappear, and the player would get to touch the screen to reveal "bonus coins" that were hidden under rocks, in treasure chests, or behind the brassieres of popular lingerie models. (Yes, I made the last one up. Good idea, though, don't you think?)

They were called "Australian-style" video slots, although it wasn't long before the American slot-makers followed suit with their own animated video games. The American slot manufacturers—starting with former pinball king Williams, now known as WMS Gaming—used the video animation and second screens to come up with their own funny cartoon bonus rounds. People began to laugh hysterically as they cheerfully lost money.

All of these changes from the 1990s are today being combined, mixed and matched, and stirred up into a mind-boggling array of choices on the slot floor. This wealth of choice confuses many players, so I'm here to tell you one overriding truth that will answer 90 percent of your questions and suspicions about how the modern slot machine decides whose money it will take and whose money it will not take:

They all operate in basically the same manner.

It's true. Regardless of which mechanical apparatus is added; regardless of how many funny cartoons there are; regardless of whether they play the song from a TV show, give the player a board game to play, play the overture from *Les Misérables,* or get down on one knee and sing "Mammy," all modern slot machines basically follow the Telnaus virtual-reel design. They are all computers. Programmers plug a bunch of numbers into a computer program, assigning more numbers to low-paying or nonpaying reel results and fewer numbers to higher-paying reel results. Random number generator software cycles through all the numbers in the program at speeds upwards of two hundred million numbers per second (and that's a conservative estimate), and selects one number the instant you hit the "spin" button or pull the handle. The RNG continues to cycle through all the numbers even when the machine is idle. The duplication in the program may weight the choices the RNG will make toward the lower-paying ones, but it is still a purely random choice—which means that any choice can theoretically result in the game's top jackpot. Even two choices in a row can hit the top prize—the machine will go through the entire set of numbers more than one hundred times in a second.

That's that. That's the way it is. That's the true poop on how slots work. That's why there is no way anyone can predict with anything approaching accuracy when a slot machine's RNG will select a winning combination. That's why it is impossible to make a reliable living as a full-time slot jockey—you can never know when that computer program is going to select a high-paying jackpot, or when it is going to drain every single penny you possess.

I tell this to people over and over again, but they still have a hard time accepting it. They hate the concept that dumb luck guides their future at anything. They think there are evil little gnomes inside the machine who make them lose.

There are no evil little gnomes making you lose. When you lose, it is because you are a bad person and God hates you.

Seriously, though, the reluctance to accept the notion of a purely random gambling device has led to a wealth of urban legends and myths concerning the slot machine, which is the subject of a chapter later on.

I had to get the gnomes in there, though, because that's what I called this chapter. I did an entire column on the gnomes once, naming them "Ralph, Nick, and George." (RNG, get it?) But I promised myself I would recycle as few of my old jokes as possible in this book. I will concentrate instead on stealing the jokes of others.

Chapter 4

Frequently High-Hitting Payback Percentage

Now that we've firmly established what a slot machine is, what a slot machine is not, what it can do, what it cannot do, and how your author has an annoying penchant for writing laboriously long sentences, it's time to analyze how you can reasonably expect these games to behave when you plunk in your disposable income, or your grocery money, or the money you had saved for little Timmy's operation.

First, let's get a bit of jargon out of the way. We gaming writers love to use jargon, because it throws up the notion that we actually know what we're talking about. For us slot "news hawks"—those of us who "pound the pavement" on the "slot beat" turning in "hot copy" to cigar-chomping "editors" and get "sloppy-ass drunk" on "expense accounts"—the two most frequently spewed chunks of jargon are "payback percentage" and "hit frequency."

Many slot players confuse these two terms, so let's set the record straight. "Payback percentage" is a number, almost always under 100, with a squiggly punctuation mark formed by a circle, a slash, and another circle ("%"), and . . .

Wait. Maybe I'm getting into too much detail here. Payback percentage is the portion of the total coins placed in a machine over the long run that is returned to players in jackpots. It is programmed into the game chip as a "theoretical percentage" at the factory as we described earlier, and is verified in an "actual percentage" through "actual play" by "actual players." Magazines such as *Casino Player* and *Strictly Slots* report these actual numbers in monthly charts. The reason they can do this is that the commercial jurisdictions all require casinos to report their monthly slot "hold" percentage by denomination. Hold percentage is the opposite of payback percentage: it's the portion of money put into slots each month that the casino holds as revenue. The magazines flip-flop those official numbers to calculate actual monthly payback percentages for each denomination.

Most jurisdictions set a minimum payback percentage all slots must meet. In New Jersey, it's 83 percent. In Nevada, it's 75 percent, also known as "payout level at the airport."

People often misinterpret this number, and are amazed that they are losing on a machine that advertises a "guaranteed" payback of 99 percent. Ninety-nine percent payback does not mean *you* win 99 cents for *every* dollar you put in. It means that, over months, or years, 99 cents of every dollar placed in the machine will be returned in jackpots to many, many players. Or maybe a few incredibly lucky jerks.

The point is, 99 percent of the money put in the game over the long run will come out as jackpots. A simpler way of looking at it is that a 99 percent payback means the house has a 1 percent edge. (That's certainly the way the house looks at it.) Even a game with 100 percent payback (it's actually possible in a few video poker games—and in change machines) doesn't mean you'll win. It simply means it's an even-money game. You have a 50/50 chance of winning. Over the long run, you will lose approximately as much as someone else wins.

"Hit frequency" refers to how that payback is distributed—to many, many players or to a few lucky jerks. The percentage reflects how often, on average, a winning combination lands on the payline or paylines. A 50 percent hit frequency means a winning combination of some kind will land approximately every other spin. Again, this is over the long term—it could be hit, miss, hit, miss; or hit, hit, miss, miss, hit, miss . . . well, you get the picture.

In general, "high hit frequency" means that the game will dribble small jackpots all the time, but now and then you'll win a few even smaller jackpots. Occasionally, a bigger win will rear its head in the primary game or in the bonus round. Most of the multiline video "Australian-style" games have high hit frequency. Most people who play them like the idea that a $20 bill will last a lot longer on this kind of game than on the traditional slots. They play and play, and watch the cartoons, and win some of their money back in the bonus round, and play some more, and eventually lose all their money. But they've really "won," you see, because of the "gaming entertainment" they have just experienced. Sure, they "lost," but it was "fun." These games are designed to, in the *actual words of an actual slot manufacturing executive*, make it *"fun to lose."*

Personally, I just have a grand time when I lose. *[SARCASM ALERT . . . SARCASM ALERT . . .]* You know, there's nothing I can think of that gives me more of a warm, fuzzy feeling than sticking that last dog-eared bill from my wallet into an acceptor and then leaving the casino sifting through the lint in my pocket like some pathetic hobo.

Casino slot managers love high hit frequency, because it gives them another bit of jargon—"low volatility." This means, basically, low risk. The jackpot levels remain relatively constant. Slot managers know that, on this type of game, the risk is small that a couple of lucky players are going to kill them with big jackpots that suck the profit from the bottom line, sending them to their superiors to beg for their jobs.

Many players think that a game with "low hit frequency" is "bad." But that's not necessarily so. The best reel-spinners have low hit frequency. You can sit spinning your reels for excruciatingly long periods without hitting a winning combination, but the tradeoff is that when you do hit something it's a nice, meaty win. The "high-rolling" gamblers love this type of game. They'll come prepared with a good bankroll, perfectly willing to wait out those dry spells for the big payoff, knowing that they are trying to outlast a house edge that's only one or two percentage points.

The casinos would love to scrap this type of game, because of its "high volatility." People can lose big, but they can also win big. On balance, the games make money because those couple of percentage points of house edge at the $1, $5, or $25 denominations translate into a ton of green pouring into the slots. But, because of that volatility factor, and because these games are generally placed in the highest denominations on the floor, the casinos are more at risk of getting slammed by a few lucky shmucks. And then having to break the news to their bosses. Slot managers can reasonably expect their jobs to be on the line, but fortunately, since the mob left the casino game shortly after Joe Pesci and Robert DeNiro got kicked out of the Tangiers, at least they no longer have to worry about being chopped up into little pieces and ending up as part of the foundation of a building somewhere in Jersey.

The vast majority of slot games out there fall into one of the two general categories described above (or below, if you're holding the book upside-down)—high hit frequency with low volatility; or low hit frequency with high volatility. Recognizing which type of game it is before you sit down is one of the keys to whether you will succeed or fail at the slot game. Knowing how a slot is going to behave makes it much easier to manage your money while you play. Here's how to recognize how your game is likely to go:

If the game has lots of paylines, an encyclopedic pay table, and funny cartoon bonus rounds, it's a good bet it will have high hit frequency. If it's a classic three-reel slot with seven or eight paying combinations and multiplying wild symbols, you can expect a low hit frequency with occasional large jackpots. If you play the first kind, expect your money to go a little further, but don't count on a lot of hundred-dollar jackpots. If you play the second kind, be prepared for a lot of bill-acceptor feedings and hope for the big score.

There are many games that tweak these two characteristics, and those are the games you have to watch out for. There are games with low hit frequency that don't give you enough large jackpots to compensate for the dry spells, and there are multiline video games with bonus rounds that don't have a high enough hit frequency. There are ways you can recognize these stinkers, and that's what we'll talk about in the next chapter.

But first, a "behind-the-scenes" look at how high-hit-frequency games came to America:

SLOT MANAGER: Boss, we're getting killed by these big jackpots.

BOSS: Well, I just saw some games down in Australia that almost never pay big jackpots.

SLOT MANAGER : Then why do people play them?

BOSS: They give the suckers [NOTE: *his* term, not mine] a lot of little jackpots to keep them going, and suck their credit meters dry a little bit at a time.

SLOT MANAGER : Then why do people keep playing them if they're losing?

BOSS: Two words: Cartoons and ATMs.

SLOT MANAGER : But that's three words.

BOSS: Shut up and go count the money.

Chapter 5

Yes,
You Can Win

Many of the scam "slot systems," which seem to proliferate from bookshelves and the Web like anal vapors after a red-bean dinner, purport to offer "guaranteed" methods of winning at the slots, *every* time. I will not tell you anything that will guarantee you a winning session on the slots.

Hey, then what the hell good *is* this book, anyway?

No, don't stop reading. This book is good. I know, because you just bought it, and someone with your obvious intelligence, good looks, and impeccable taste in literature would never buy a useless book. Your friends know this too, and they will shower you with adulation after you tell them each to go out and buy several copies of this book. You can set a good example right now by marching back to the bookstore and buying, say, a hundred more copies.

Go ahead; I'll wait.

[CHEERY WHISTLING AND FINGER-TAPPING]

Back already? Good.

The reason I will not give you a guaranteed method of winning at the slots is that no such method exists. Well, there is one—you could take a sledgehammer, smash the front of a machine to smithereens, grab all the money, and run. The only caveat is that I'm fairly certain casinos frown on this type of activity.

As I have repeated *ad nauseum* (literally, "until you want to puke"), there is no way to guarantee a winning session on the slots. However, there are ways to minimize your losses, thus maximizing the chance that you will walk away from the slots with more cash than when you arrived. The tips I will give you in this chapter can ultimately determine whether you are going to end your slot session dining on the fine gourmet fare of victory or noshing gloomily on the grease-stained cheese steak of despair.

(That's right, Mr. Barry. I can do metaphors too.)

So how can you give yourself the best possible chance to walk away from the slot floor as a winner? The answer, of course, is to play craps or blackjack.

No, I'm "engaging in tomfoolery" again. Here is my personal recipe for the type of long-term success at the slots that I can't guarantee. No, wait. That didn't come out right. What I mean is here is how to avoid going broke, and how to maximize your chance of bucking that big house edge on the slot games.

The first thing you want to remember is to *know your game*. Know it *inside and out*. And in *italics*. Before you can do that, you need to determine just what it is you like about playing slots. Do you play for fun? Or do you play for the thrill of gambling and the chance to win some big bucks? Decide whether you want to play a high-hit-frequency game for the sheer entertainment of it—win or lose—or to get down and dirty and try to win some serious cash, even if you have to fork out some hefty wagers to do it.

Use that little nugget of advice I dished out in the last chapter to find the type of game you like. Let's say you go for the high-hit-frequency variety, a multiline video slot that is chock full of "gaming entertainment." (The word "gaming," by the way, was created by the casino industry to replace the word "gambling," with all its negative connotations. It comes from the Latin word *gam*, which means "to dump money down the toilet.") Most of these games offer frequent little hits, but take a few minutes to check out the help screen before you play. Look for the winning combinations that look exciting, but which only pay a pittance (or maybe a pittance and sixpence) for lining up five of them. Look for the big winners in the pay table. As you begin playing, make a mental note of exactly what your "frequent hits" are.

Oh, and quit sloshing down those bourbon-and-sodas, or you won't be able to make a mental note of anything, including your name.

Chances are, this will be a nickel game, or even a penny or two-cent game that takes, like, a thousand credits and pays out in tickets. There's a method to this small-denomination madness—smaller denominations mean lots and lots of credits, in wins that "look" big but really are not. That's how they keep the excitement going on this kind of game. It is also how they bamboozle you out of your money. Bells will ring, funny little music will play, and the screen will say "WINNER!!" And then, if you do the math, you'll realize you've won about three bucks. ("Look, Madge! I just won two million farthings!")

As you play, keep an eye on your credit meter. If you keep seeing "WINNER!" and hearing cute music and watching funny cartoons, but the credit meter keeps going down, guess what? *You're really LOSING!* A good rule of thumb is that, if you go through an entire $20 bill on a nickel game without your credit meter going *up,* move on to another game. You may not be able to afford much more fun and frivolity.

Many of these multiline video slots make up for all the tiny little hits in the primary game by offering a lucrative bonus round. And that's just fine—many people play this type of game strictly for the bonus anyway. But here's the thing—you should actually *get to the bonus round* once in a while. More and more video slots these days advertise gargantuan bonus awards, but you have to pay out the nose to even get a shot at winning.

HUSBAND: I just won three hundred dollars in the bonus round!

WIFE: Great! How long have you been playing?

HUSBAND : It will be three months this Tuesday. By the way, I just took out a second mortgage on the house.

WIFE : It's a third mortgage. I took out the second last week. But I'm expecting a bonus round myself any day now.

HUSBAND : Shweet!

Here's an astonishing revelation: If you never see the bonus round, it's not a "bonus." It is a stinker. Again, use the $20 method—

if Jackson goes into the bill acceptor on a nickel game and you play it through without seeing the bonus, don't put another dead president into the slot. Move on.

You will occasionally win big jackpots on a multiline video slot. It does happen. It's happened to me many times. The big wins are in there; you'll just hit the little "dribble wins" a lot more. When the juicy jackpot does come on a multiline video slot, *take the money and skeedaddle*. Meaty jackpots are rare enough in the multiline genre that hitting one should almost always be a cash-out event. Quit playing for a while. Go have dinner. *You won!* You have successfully bucked the house odds. If you keep playing, you're just going to give it all back. You know it, I know it, and, most importantly, the casino knows it.

Print that ticket out. If there's no ticket printer, hit the cash-out button and wait for the inevitable "Hopper Empty—Call Attendant" signal, wait roughly a day for the new sack of coins, scoop them all up, and use your grimy paws to lug those coin buckets across the floor.

Of course, if you're playing these games for sheer entertainment, you may not care about giving the money back. A lot of these new games are packed with entertainment, and there's nothing wrong with playing for fun. Just make sure you're getting enough fun for your money—a nice long play session for a relatively small investment.

My favorite "play for fun" games are the ones packed with a variety of bonus features: the Monopoly series by WMS, the Ripley's games from Mikohn, and Trivial Pursuit. I love that one. I love answering trivia questions, and I always have fun on these games, even if I do end up losing money in the end. The key to enjoyment in all of these games, though, is that bonus rounds are kicking in left and right. They're all really frequent. I end up playing a good, long time. And I even *learn* stuff while I play. Like, I learned in one of the Ripley's trivia questions that "Face-Slapping" was a legitimate sport in Russia during the Soviet era.

That's the type of knowledge that can change your life.

Yes, playing for fun is just fine, but just make sure your "fun" doesn't clean you out, and remember one overriding truth: It is always more fun to win than to lose.

I've got to admit, though, when I play slots, I go mostly for the money, and I mostly play the old, tried-and-true reel-spinners. I play

Blazing 7s, in the "Diamond Line" version. I play Double Diamond. I play Five Times Pay and Ten Times Pay. I love hitting those multiplying wild symbols for the big jackpots. There are far too many times I give it back, but there are enough times I walk away a winner that I keep going back to them. I love that adrenaline rush, particularly on the dollar games.

So how do you maximize your chances of walking away a winner when playing the traditional reel-spinners? One word: bankroll. Oh, and patience. (Okay, *two* words, wise guy.) You've got to sit down at this type of game prepared to go through some money in your quest for the big hit. You're not going to get those friendly little dribble hits every other spin. You're going to hit dry spells here and there. But they will be punctuated, with a little luck, by some beefy wins. And I live for the beefy wins.

The key is not to get your Jockeys rumpled if you go through a couple of bills without a big hit. Sit down with a big enough bankroll to weather a few dry spells in your quest. The big hits will come, and they'll usually be a lot bigger than those hits you got on the multiline video slot.

Of course, maybe they won't come in this session. The key to success, and to sanity, in playing a volatile reel-spinner is to sit down with a bankroll that you are completely prepared to lose. You may lose it tonight and gain it back tomorrow. You may not get it back this trip. That's what gambling is all about. If you want to play in the big reel-spinning leagues, play what you can afford to lose. Sure, you might lose, but one of these times you're going to score the big hit. In this type of game, the thrill is in the chase.

I am often asked how much of a bankroll is appropriate for a casino trip of this length or that length. My answer is always the same: It depends on what kind of game you're playing, the denomination you wager, and what you can honestly lose without surrendering to the ever-present "ATM impulse." I can tell you, though, what I have found to be an appropriate bankroll in my own experience: I use the "kin and cain't method." I play as long as I kin, and, when my pocket's empty, I cain't.

No, seriously, if I'm settling in for a night at the multiline video slots—nickel games with high hit frequency and lots of bonus rounds—anywhere from $60 to $100 will get me through an entire night, providing the games are decent. There have been nights when

I have found a single $20 bill ended up getting me through the entire night, and I've walked away ahead of the game. But a C-note is usually more than enough for hours and hours of play, and usually you can spend a lot less and have a good time on an entertaining nickel video slot.

If I'm going for the gold on traditional reel-spinners, I won't sit down to play quarters for more than an hour without at least a hundred dollars. Usually, three hundred dollars will give me enough to weather all the dry spells in a good, long play session. In these instances, I usually either end up with a big win, or with an impulse to ask passing pedestrians for spare change.

Playing dollars is a whole other kettle of fish. If I have several hundred to begin with, maybe I'll test my luck with a hundred dollars on a dollar game. Sometimes, a big hit will land and my stake will go up to three or four hundred dollars in an instant, and I'll settle in for a good session of dollar play. Other times, the C-note will be gone in minutes, and I'll go back down to quarter reel-spinners or nickel video slots. If I'm bound and determined to play dollars all night, I figure I'd better have a bankroll at the outset of at least five hundred dollars—or, perhaps more realistically, a thousand—which I'm prepared to lose in that quest for the big payoff. Remember, a hundred-dollar bill on a dollar game buys you the same number of spins as $25 does on a quarter game. And, in the traditional reels, $25 in quarters requires the intangible—luck—for success.

There are entire books offering suggestions for how to stretch your bankroll and how to manage your money at the slots. The best tips on success at the slots, in fact, almost always relate in some way to money management. Many experts will tell you to put your bankroll for each day of your trip in a separate envelope, and, when your envelope for the day is empty, quit playing. If you have that kind of discipline, go for it. But remember this—the method only works if you take *one envelope* with you to the casino. Leave the rest in your room. If they're all in your pockets, you'll want to dip into tomorrow's envelope when today's is empty, just to see if your luck is going to be any better in the future, and before you know it you're looking at four days of watching *Oprah* in a hotel room.

The key to money management lies in being honest with yourself. How much can you honestly afford to lose in a day? Knowing when to quit is absolutely the most difficult decision to make in a casino, particularly when you know that any single spin can theoretically hit a jackpot. I've found that luck is either with me early or not at all. If I'm winning, it's fun, and, if I'm having fun, I keep playing. If I'm losing consistently enough to sink into that greasy cheese steak of despair, and I start to hate the machine, the cocktail waitress, the big goof sitting next to me who's winning, and life itself, it's time to head back to the room and watch a movie. Otherwise, I'm chasing losses—and chasing losses is the shortest route to the top of the parking garage for the Rooftop Diving Competition (a popular Olympic event in Atlantic City).

All right, now you know what to expect from the different kinds of slot games, and how to have the best chance of bucking the odds. That's if you've been listening attentively to all I've said in this chapter. I hope you were paying attention.

Especially to the part about going out and buying a hundred more copies of this book.

Oh well, on to the next chapter. But give me a minute. For some reason, I've just *got* to go out and get a cheese steak, with extra grease.

Chapter 6

You Can't Be Serious

Take all the popular myths you've ever heard—Santa Claus, the Easter Bunny, the Lost Continent of Atlantis, Homeland Security—put them all together, and they will not even come close to the number of myths that abound concerning the modern slot machine.

If all the myths about slots were true, you could go into a casino with a blow torch and heat up a bunch of coins, alternate pulling the handle and pushing the spin button, and walk away a winner every time. But you wouldn't even have to do that, because you could just look for someone who is losing consistently, and sit down as soon as he gets up, and hit a jackpot. Or go to the machine on the end of an aisle and clean up because they're the loosest games in the house. Or just pay off the shifty-eyed Italian guy in the silk suit, black shirt, and white tie (that would be me), and he'll flip the "pay-out switch" for your machine.

There are people who actually believe all of the myths that have developed concerning the slot machine. Depending on the myth, their belief ranges from completely understandable to downright scary.

But there's no need to worry, because Mr. Frank the Answer Man is here with the facts to dispel all of those nasty myths and urban legends (What the hell *is* an urban legend, anyway? Are there rural legends too?) about the modern slot. Here are my personal Top 12 Slot Myths. I was going to do a Top 10, but I wanted to be a "rebel." A "maverick." A "numbskull."

I'll take on the myths one at a time, in single file, one after the other, again and again, on and on, blah blah blah, and smash them all to smithereens, figuratively, literally, and puckishly. (I just learned that word.)

Myth No. 1

"I was losing for three hours, and got up to go to the bathroom. A guy sat down at my slot and hit a jackpot on the first pull. He stole my jackpot!"

Reality No. 1

You should know better than to "get up to go to the bathroom." You should always wear Huggies when you play slots.

The guy did not "steal your jackpot." It is virtually impossible. Think about it. There are only one or two numbers that correspond to that top jackpot, out of thousands of numbers in the program. The random number generator cycles through all the numbers over one hundred times every second. That means the chance that you would have hit that same jackpot is . . . well, trust me, it's *really* tiny. Plus, you would have had to hit the spin button at the exact same nanosecond that he hit it, which is probably another one-in-a-gazillion chance. To think that he stole your jackpot is to accept the notion that you are quite possibly the unluckiest person on the entire planet.

The chance that he stole your jackpot is roughly equivalent to the chance that Americans will soon embrace the metric system, or ever understand what a "wind chill factor" actually is. (My theory is that there is a guy at every TV station who walks outside and says, "It's 40 degrees? Damn! Feels like 20!" and another guy writes it down. But, again, I digress. . . .)

No, the guy didn't steal your jackpot, but he did steal your seat. And he did win, and you lost. So you're allowed to hate him. He's probably a jerk anyway.

Myth No. 2

"When business is slow, the casino flips a switch to make the payback percentages on the slots higher. When the casino is busy, they flip the switch back to lower percentages."

Reality No. 2

Right. And if too many people are winning and the payout switch guy is sick, they just flood the casino with anti-payout fairy dust.

Believe it or not, there is no payout switch. There is no computer program hooked up to all the machines that casinos use to alter payback percentages. The payback percentages are governed by the way the numbers are fed into the program at the slot factory (owned, of course, by Willie Wonka). These number sets are written into various game chips that go into the slot machines. The manufacturers offer slot games to the casinos with five or six possible programs, each with a separate theoretical payback percentage, each on a separate chip (available in flavors ranging from Mesquite Barbecue to Nacho Cheese). These have been checked both internally and by regulatory agencies when a game is in the approval process for each jurisdiction.

The way they check it is by running a simulation of millions and millions of individual spins—they simulate play over the expected life of the machine, which is usually five years. Then they simulate getting a free buffet and Frank Sinatra tickets. (I know, he's dead. But these are simulated tickets.)

When the machines are installed, the payback chips are verified by regulatory officials using handheld computers. (I think they also have Game Boy on them.) Once the game chips are installed on the circuit boards and locked into the machines, they cannot be replaced without a regulatory official present, often wearing a bad suit. If two or more programs are purchased for any game, the extra game chips are kept under lock and key, and regulators have to be notified if the casino intends to change the percentage chip.

These are the rules, and casinos follow them because they value the licenses that permit them to legally take your money. Again, think about it: Slots are already a huge gravy train for the casinos. While the most popular table games yield a house edge of maybe 2 or 3 percent, slots typically have a 10 percent house edge. Casinos will not risk losing their legal right to rake in millions to play with a couple of percentage points.

Even if they did want to alter payback percentages according to business, it would involve sending a fleet of attendants out to physically change the chips in thousands of machines. Several times in a day or a week. If you think they have that kind of manpower, just think about how long it takes you to find an attendant to get a sack of coins over to your machine when the hopper is empty. I've seen seasons change, international régimes topple, and several species evolve in the time it takes to get an attendant to drag a sack of quarters across the floor.

For that matter, casinos don't normally buy extra game chips, because they're expensive. They buy one chip with each game. If too many people win money on a game, they don't change the percentage. They change the game. It's a lot less hassle.

Myth No. 3

"I was winning, and my machine malfunctioned. An attendant did something inside the machine to fix it, and then I started losing. He changed the payout percentage!"

Reality No. 3

That's what you get for whining about your game being broken. Seriously, though, you were able to find an attendant?

See above. Weren't you paying attention? I'm not going to go through all that stuff again about how payback percentages are set at the factory. If you missed it, you'll have to copy somebody else's notes. And stop chewing gum in my class!

Slot attendants do not carry game chips around with them. They're lucky the casino lets them have tools. They can't change the percentage on a machine when they open the door, any more than they can answer a question like "Where's the closest bathroom?" without sending you to a bathroom in a neighboring county.

To put it as tactfully as possible, slot attendants don't give a rat's ass whether you win or lose. They just want to fix your machine as quickly as possible, and move on to the next whiny player. And they want a tip. If they could change the payout percentage in the machine, they'd change it to make you win, not lose. And then they'd want a tip.

Myth No. 4

"I tipped a change person to tell me where the hot machines were. He/she showed me a game that hadn't been paying for a long time—it was "due."

Reality No. 4

Congratulations. You are a schmuck.

Unless the slot attendant was a psychic, you just wasted your money. It is impossible for anyone to predict when a machine is "due" for a jackpot. I don't care if a machine has awarded 20 jackpots in a row—it means nothing with respect to the next spin.

Remember, the RNG is cycling through hundreds of millions of numbers per second, and it keeps cycling when the machine is idle. It is random, dumb luck where the computer will be in its cycling at any given time. Therefore, it can turn out losing numbers for weeks and still turn out losing numbers for another week. Or it can hit a jackpot on the next spin. Or it can hit 20 jackpots on the next 20 spins. No one can know for sure what it will do next (except for the fact that it will always run out of coins when you cash out).

One possible exception could be a progressive link that has been in place for a long time, where the prize is larger than it ever has been. If an attendant or change person is very familiar with the jackpot neighborhood in which that progressive has consistently hit over months or years, and the link is packed with players overcome with jackpot fever (it does go around), it may be a self-fulfilling prophecy that someone will soon hit the jackpot—more players playing faster increases the odds that someone will hit the jackpot.

But don't bet the farm on it. It still doesn't guarantee anyone is going to hit it today, tomorrow, or next week. And there is no one, regardless of how long he/she has been working in that area, who can tell you with certainty that a progressive is ready to hit. Join in the jackpot fever if you want, but don't be surprised if you end up visiting the ATM instead of shopping for yachts.

Finally, it's a good idea to steer clear of anyone who can be identified as a "he/she."

Myth No. 5

"Casinos always place the loosest machines on the ends of rows, so people can be seen winning."

Reality No. 5

No, it's so the casino "suits" can see people winning. And break their legs.

This one's been around for a long time, and it may have been true at some point. But it's also one of the most well-known and widespread notions about where casinos place the loose machines. So why on earth would they do it?

The reality is that casinos sprinkle high-paying machines in with lower-paying machines all over the floor. But, even so, the differences in payback percentages are minuscule within one given denomination. Payback percentages are a matter of casino policy. Slot managers will stick to one general payback number for nickels, a higher one for quarters, an even higher one for dollars. So one quarter machine is likely to be just as loose or tight as the next quarter machine.

Incidentally, the nickel percentage number for reels is going to be much lower than the nickel number for multiline video slots. They go by average wager when they decide on a policy for a given type of machine. Average bets on a 45-coin nickel game are normally around the same as on a three-coin quarter game—and so are the payback percentages. Other than this one exception, percentages are almost always consistent among various games in a given denomination.

And, what's more, those percentages are figured out over the long term—millions and millions of spins, as verified on handheld payback percentage/Game Boy computers. Anything can happen in the short term. You can win on a machine that has 90 percent payback; you can lose on a machine that has 99 percent payback. It all depends on whether the luck gods are with you that day.

What I'm trying to say, in a painfully roundabout manner, is this: don't knock yourself out trying to figure where the loose machines are placed. If you're lucky, you'll win; if you're unlucky, you'll lose. That's why they call it gambling.

And, besides, if you think the casino places the loose machines on the end, they'll put them second from the end, because they think you think they're on the end. And if they know you think they think you think they're on the end, then they'll put them on the end, because you think they think you know they think . . . Oh, never mind!

Myth No. 6

"When I go into the 'pick-a-tile' bonus round on a video slot, the result is predetermined, so it doesn't matter which tile I pick."

Reality No. 6

Video slot bonus rounds in different games have common features, like showing you a hilarious cartoon so you laugh while every penny is being sucked out of your wallet. (More on this later. Film at 11.)

But another thing common in all the "pick-a-tile" bonus games—the ones that show you five rocks, or five treasure chests, or five severed heads, and ask you to pick three for hidden bonus amounts—is that the RNG makes a selection of bonus amounts when the bonus round is triggered.

However, the RNG selects an *entire screen* of bonus amounts. All that is predetermined is the amount behind each of the severed heads. It's up to you to find the severed heads hiding the highest bonuses.

So it *does* matter which one you pick. Some games even show you the ones you didn't pick, just in case you picked the lowest amounts and need to experience a little useless grief. It's the equivalent of the computer saying, "*Nyaa*-nyaa!"

Myth No. 7

"By counting the number of spaces and symbols on the reels in relation to the award for each winning combination, someone with skill at mathematics can determine the odds on a reel-spinning game."

Reality No. 7

If I want to have fun in a casino, it's not going to come from doing math.

In the past, there were actually slot professionals—mathematicians who started with the premise that there were 22 or 25 stops on each reel and, counting the symbols and blanks and mapping where they stopped in the pay window with each spin, could calculate the odds of each winning combination, and, using the pay table, could estimate the overall payback percentage on a reel-spinning slot machine. They could thus find the most favorable odds and win consistently by playing the loosest machines.

Don't ask me exactly how they did this. I get a headache just describing it.

While watching my favorite TV show, *CSI*, the other day, I realized that there are still people who do this. The show is set in Vegas, and one of the "perps" (cop-talk for "human scum") was sitting at a slot mapping out the reel results in this manner. The *CSI* guy commented that he was involved in a useless exercise.

The *CSI* guy was right, and not just because he's on TV. With the invention of the Telnaus virtual-reel system, the physical reels on a traditional slot machine became nothing more than display mechanisms. The fact that there are 22 or 25 physical spots on which a reel can stop now means nothing with respect to the number of reel results that can possibly land on any given spin. The RNG picks a number to determine the reel result. Any given physical stop on the reels can have a hundred or a thousand numbers assigned to it. Remember? It's a simulation of a 10-foot reel strip.

The computer, in fact, picks the results on a modern reel-spinner in exactly the same manner it picks results in a video slot. The physical reels perform the same function as a video screen—to display the result chosen by the RNG.

You can no longer gain anything by looking at the physical reels of a slot machine, mapping results, and then doing math—except maybe carpal tunnel syndrome.

And it's just as well. I wouldn't want to frequent a casino full of people who, when asked what they'd like to do for a fun night out, say, "Math!"

Myth No. 8

"If the reels wiggle, it means the machine is getting ready to pay out."

Reality No. 8

You're not listening, dammit!

The reels are display mechanisms. Just like a video screen. I don't care if they wiggle, go faster, go slower, do jumping jacks or fly out of the machine and hit you in the head. It doesn't mean the machine is getting ready to pay.

Maybe if the reels said, "I'm getting ready to pay," they would be getting ready to pay. But I have yet to hear of that happening.

Myth No. 9

"If I have my slot club card inserted, the game pays less."

Reality No. 9

The slot club card is in no way linked to the RNG. It is there so the casino can track you down if you win, and kill you.

Seriously, though, there is absolutely no relationship between the slot club card and the computer's selection of winning results. The slot club is there for your benefit. It is there so the casino can identify who is giving them the most "action," and "reward" them by giving them "key chains." More importantly, it is tracking how much you wager and awarding you cash back according to how much you are betting.

That's why you should never, ever play any slot machine without the club card inserted. If you don't use the card, you will get no credit for being a loyal customer.

And you won't have any casino key chains, either.

Myth No. 10

"If I heat up the coins, it will affect the payout mechanism to cause a jack-pot. The same thing happens if I freeze the coins."

Reality No. 10

If you believe this one, perhaps it is time to seek some sort of professional help, such as electroshock therapy. Or maybe a frontal lobotomy would do the trick. (Bonus joke: I'd rather have a bottle in front of me than a frontal lobotomy.)

I have read of instances in which people actually burned their fingers by trying to heat coins up with lighters before putting them in the slot. I have also read that people have brought coolers into the casino to chill their coins before inserting them.

I have tried to explain how slots make their choices of winning or losing combinations. Heating or cooling the coins will do one of two things: make them hot or make them cold. They will sit there in the coin mechanism, being either hot or cold, until you push the button or pull the handle. Then the RNG will select a number.

Correction: heating or cooling coins will do one more thing—it will help gaming writers working on books pinpoint the complete morons on a slot floor, and then write about them.

Myth No. 11

"The RNG's decision depends on how many coins I wager."

Reality No. 11

Wrong. The RNG's decision depends on how attractive you are.

At one time, way back in the 1980s, the RNGs in slot machines would make their selection when you dropped the first coin in the slot. Nowadays, the decision on the reel result is made the instant you hit the spin button or pull the handle.

Either way, the RNG's decision is not dependent on how many coins you put in the slot, or how many coins you erase from your credit meter. It's a computer. It doesn't say to itself, "I'm going to give this cheap nitwit a small jackpot because he only bet one measly coin." It is a bunch of wires and microprocessor chips, and it's almost certain that it has no opinions of its own. It doesn't care how cheap you are; it doesn't care how much you bet.

Now, it *is* true that the RNG will make a different decision if you bet two coins than if you bet one. But the amount of the bet is not the determining factor—it is the time it took you to insert that extra coin. Remember, the RNG is cycling through two hundred million numbers per second. That means that, even if you're using the credit button to play, the time it takes to hit the bet button one more time will cause a different selection than it would make if one credit is played.

The question of when the RNG makes its selection is one that confounds many, and the various opinions on this subject all beg one question:

Why on Earth do you care?

It is a random choice out of millions of possible choices, regardless of when the RNG makes that decision. Even if it makes a different choice with two coins in as opposed to one, it's not necessarily a better or worse choice.

So quit worrying about it. Life is too short. (But keep asking me about it. I have to make a living.)

Myth No. 12

"If I alternate pushing the button and pulling the handle, it increases my chance of winning."

Reality No. 12

Won't work. You've got to touch the screen and say "wiener-schnitzel" between pushing and pulling.

The "push-and-pull" is a popular ritual, and it's fun, in a sort of obsessive-compulsive kind of way. But it doesn't do anything to affect the RNG's choice. That's partly because the handle on a slot is now a useless appendage, like a necktie, or Dick Cheney. Back in the days when slots were mechanical, pulling the handle actually did something—it loaded springs which, when released, sent the reels spinning, causing the user to say curse words when the reels stopped. But now, the handle is just there for the sake of nostalgia.

There are still springs, to make it feel like you're winding the reels up when you pull the handle. But all the handle does is touch a switch to signal the RNG to choose a number. So when you pull the handle instead of pushing the spin button, all you're actually doing is making the handle push its own spin button.

I'm not saying you shouldn't do the old push-and-pull, or touch the screen, or punch your fist on the console to summon luck. We all have our little rituals that we do while we gamble. It's part of what makes casino gambling fun.

Personally, I have found that if you walk around your chair, spit on the floor, spell out "R-A-G-G-M-O-P-P" three times, sing the theme song to *The Patty Duke Show,* and hit the spin button with your pinkie toe, it results in a sure jackpot every time.

(All together now: *But they're cousins . . . identical cousins, all the way . . .*)

Chapter 7

But I've Got a System

Okay, okay . . . that last little joke in my "myth" chapter was pretty funny, wasn't it? And I'll just bet that you knew I was joking right away, didn't you?

But there is one genre of, umm, "literature" in which I could sell a statement like "Singing the theme song to *The Patty Duke Show* will cause your slot machine to hit a jackpot every time, as long as you pick your nose and bug your eyes out like Barney Fife as you sing." I could slap it together with a bunch of other preposterous statements between a couple of pieces of blue paper, and sell it to you for $29.99 over the Internet. And you know what? *A lot of people would buy it.*

They would buy it because I wouldn't tell them up front about Barney Fife and Patty Duke. I would set up a fancy Web site that said, "I have a *secret system* to beat the slots! I can't tell you about it now because it's secret. It's so secret even *I* don't know it! But I got these secrets from a guy who used to build slot machines, and fix slot machines, and, in fact, he's the guy who *invented* slot machines, and he knows all the secret 'glitches' in them, which he put there so he could go out and beat them himself, except that he got sent to prison first, but he gave them to me because I let him sleep with my wife, but

I'll give them to you right now because I hate the casinos and I want you to win and you want to win, but first you have to give me $29.99."

Okay, maybe I'm exaggerating, but only in the part about offering a prisoner conjugal visits with my wife. As incredible as it may seem, there are *a lot* of dirtbags out there who will try to sell you a bill of goods that has claims very similar to those in the sales pitch. They are all scams, scams, scams, and I am here to tell you that, if you are willing to plunk down money and send away for a "secret system" to beat the slots, you may as well just take $29.99, put it in a paper bag, bury it in your backyard, and wait for it to sprout into a money tree. Because your likelihood of getting rich from this procedure is exactly the same as if you sent away for a secret slot system.

I have described the way slots work, but the truth is, most people do not know how they work. Consequently, they will believe anything that sounds reasonable if they think it will give them a better chance to win. They will even believe stuff that doesn't sound reasonable—as evidenced by the fact that these bloodthirsty sharks sell lots of these systems to poor, unsuspecting chum.

Before researching this book, I had never actually sent away for a secret slot system, mainly because I knew how slots work, and thus I never believed any of the Internet sales pitches. Once I had an author send me his "secret" slot-system book because he wanted me to plug it in one of my columns. He said he had made millions playing slots and had the W2G forms to prove it. I told him winning tax-reportable jackpots only proves that he happened to be lucky and maybe that he had a big bankroll, but that I would look the system over anyway. I went through the whole thing with a fine-tooth comb (this was when I had hair and still owned fine-tooth combs), and wrote the guy back and told him he was a lousy scam artist who was bilking honest people out of their money. He did challenge me to a public test of his system, but I told him I had real work to do and did not wish to engage in fantasy pursuits.

I have looked over many "literary" works purporting to guarantee success at the slots, but never any that approached a basis in fact. They all belong in the same literary category as *Harry Potter*. They are fiction.

But, for the purposes of this book, I actually did go out and gather some fresh fiction. I went on the Web looking for all the "secret systems" I could find, and I spent real money and bought a few of them. Of course, I can write off that real money as research expenses—but you can't, so I'm going to save you from wasting your own money, on these nuggets of manure. (Hey, it's the kind of guy I am.)

I will tell you first about the sales pitches so you will know how to spot the scams.

I was careful to do an Internet search including the word "guaranteed." If you see a Web site or get junk mail (some of these cats find mailing lists of good slot players) offering you a "guaranteed method" of winning at the slots, trash it immediately. Slots are random, dumb luck—you can play them smart and minimize your losses, but there are no guarantees.

I also used the word "secret" in the search. All of these systems are secret. If they weren't secret, they tell you, the casinos would be out of business. But for a price, you see, you can exploit the casinos for your own benefit, and, if you simply use discretion and go from casino to casino, never hitting the same place repeatedly, you can get rich and the casinos will never catch on.

The sales pitches will attempt to lure you in by saying the author has "insider" information. It's almost always attributed to a slot mechanic, or someone who actually designs and programs slots for a living. Some will say they stumbled upon a "glitch" in the programming of *all* slot machines that no one knows about; others will say that an "industry insider" revealed secrets about the way winning combinations are programmed, or about how to tell when a slot is ready to hit a jackpot.

The pitches will never be specific about just what the author has discovered; they'll say only that it is guaranteed to give you long-term success at the slots. The pitches will be written in snake-oil-salesman language designed to entice you to take one small step to financial security—to send them $12, or $30, or whatever, saying to yourself, "Hey, what do I have to lose?"

What you have to lose, my friend, is your $12, or $30, or whatever.

Knowing all of this ahead of time, I went ahead and sent for a few systems. I'm not going to give you the exact titles, but I will tell you what I was told I was paying for in the case of the two most ludicrous "secret systems," what I ended up getting in the mail, and what I ended up getting from the slot machines while using the systems—which was nothing.

In the first system I bought, the author said he had a "slot mechanic friend" who gave him "inside trade secrets" that allowed him to develop a simple method to beat the slots. All I had to do to start "winning, winning, winning" was to send in a check for $27.99.

Now, in the real world of reputable publishing, $27.99 will usually buy you a pretty nice quality of book. You would expect a couple hundred pages with pictures and illustrations, bound in an attractive package. In this case, my $27.99 got me 22 typewritten pages between two pieces of green construction paper, bound with two staples. It included fantastic graphics consisting of photocopies of pictures of slot machines. I mean, the production cost must have been astronomical—I'm talking, like, *at least* 75 cents.

Ah, but this is going to make me rich, right? Who cares if it looks like a second-grade report on ant farms? It's the information I'm paying for. Well, in this case, the quality of the information made the production quality look like a leather-bound first-edition copy of *War and Peace:* it was chock-full of useless garbage.

The "secret system" in this case was to watch the patterns of the bar symbols and top jackpot symbols on classic reel-spinning slot machines. If the bar symbols lined up across the reels like stairs, or in an "X" formation, that was supposed to mean a big jackpot was coming soon. On the other hand, if you saw two jackpot symbols, it meant the next spin was going to be a loser. So, any time you saw two jackpot symbols, you were supposed to revert to wagering one coin on the next spin, but if you saw the magic bar-symbol patterns, you were to immediately go to max-coin for the next five spins, because a big jackpot was sure to come.

Now, I knew this was absolute hogwash without even trying it. The slot machine's random number generator program cycles through the *entire set* of possible reel results hundreds of times a second. If you see these supposed "positive combinations" of bar symbols, by the time you hit the button for your next spin the RNG has cycled through every possible combination many, many times. Any pattern of symbols you see on any given spin has absolutely no relation to what you will get on the next spin.

Still, I tried the "magic system" out. I found a traditional Double Diamond slot, and followed the system religiously. Guess what happened? I lost! Surprise, surprise! Not only did I lose, but I also repeatedly felt like an idiot when I dropped my bet down to one coin because the next spin was supposed to be a loser, and it turned out to be a winner. There were at least five times during the session that I sat there looking at a triple-bar or double-bar win for which I had only wagered a single coin. I felt like a knucklehead. The system didn't work for one simple reason, which I already knew: *it can't work.*

I figure the author must have gotten his "slot mechanic friend" mixed up with his "auto mechanic friend," and mistakenly published a method for guaranteeing better gas mileage or something. Either that, or the guy's a low-life, weasel scam artist.

Which one do you think is right?

The next system I bought was just as ridiculous, except that it only cost $12, and it used better-quality, blue construction paper for the cover. It had clip-art in it too, and there were 32 typewritten pages instead of 22, and I think the staples were more expensive. Such a deal!

The enticements in the sales pitch were the same—"insider" information from people who work in the industry. As for the information in the system, there *was* one big difference from the first book: this system had information in it that was actually valid—*over 20 years ago.* This guy actually reprinted, "by permission," a system for beating the slots that was copyrighted *in 1982.* If you have been paying attention (and we'll have a quiz on this later), you know that the virtual-reel system governing how modern slots make their selections of reel results was not yet perfected in 1982, and would not be patented until two years after this system was written. For $12 (plus the extra $6 I paid for "rush delivery"), I got a perfectly valid method for maximizing my winnings on electromechanical slot machines that no longer exist, except in museums and private collections. As for any machine you will actually find in a casino, the method is useless.

Right off the bat, you suspect something is fishy in this system when the author talks about "all those *silver dollars* clanging into the hopper." Gee, maybe I'll win a five-dollar gold piece! Or some Confederate money! Then it says, "the number of reels on a slot machine is the single most important determining factor in establishing your probability of winning or losing." Twenty-five years ago, this was true. But, since the mid-1980s, the number of reels on a slot means nothing. It can have three, six, one, or no reels—they are only display mechanisms to show the result at which the computer has arrived, the same as a video screen.

The author reprinted a second method, this one telling you how to spot a machine that is "ready" to hit a jackpot. It presents a formula to figure out your chance of hitting a jackpot in any given pull by multiplying the symbols and reels, and counting the spins to determine when a slot is most likely to be ready to hit the big payoff.

This one was copyrighted in 1981. Again, when it was originally published, this was a valid method of figuring odds on slots. But with the virtual-reel system the number of physical symbols on a reel is meaningless. It is a *simulation* of a 10-foot reel strip, with effectively as many symbols as the programmer wants to simulate.

I can't believe this is being bought and sold as a valid system for playing slots. This guy gathered a couple of 20-year-old systems, got permission to reprint them, and is making money from people who have no idea how modern slot machines actually work.

These are only a couple examples of the garbage that may come to you over the Web. There are many other "secret systems," and they will all contain something that sounds logical to you if you don't know how slots work, and many will be enticing enough that you think you may as well give it a try. That's how these people make their money—they give fancy-sounding sales pitches to people looking for *anything* to help them buck the big house edge on slots, and ask you for money without divulging anything about their systems. Then, for your $20 or $30, they'll send you a mimeographed pamphlet of useless information that cost them about 50 cents to slap together.

If anyone tells you they have a secret method that guarantees you will win on a slot machine, don't buy it. You are just lining the pockets of a slimy individual.

Of course, this doesn't mean *every* slot product you see advertised is a scam. There are good books and software products out there to help you win. (In addition to this one, I mean.) Not that I'm suggesting in any way that you would ever, ever need any other information on slot machines after reading this book, but, hey, there are some good products out there, and these guys need to make a living too. Check out Frank Scoblete's *Break the One-Armed Bandits*, which contains good, useful, and extremely well-written information on how to maximize your chances of walking away from the slot floor as a winner. Frank is—as are all people named "Frank"—truly a great writer, with a snappy wit played out in lively prose. And the guy knows his stuff.

And, of course, I'm not saying this just because that book is from the same publisher as this one, or because Frank is my editor for this book and most assuredly has guaranteed that the product you hold in your hand is exactly, word-for-word, as I submitted it in the manuscript. Frank's expertise is for real. (So *obviously*, he's not going make a silly mistake like changing a single word I've written, right? Well, *duh!*)

Another good slot book is John Robison's *The Slot Expert's Guide to Winning at Slots.* John is a mathematician, and he knows slots inside and out. He can tell you how the laws of mathematical probabilities work in slot machines, and he approaches everything about the modern slot from a position of knowledge.

There's even good slot stuff available on the Web, like Steve Gibbs' *Casino Gambling Exposed.* This is an "e-book" that contains a lot of good information on increasing your odds of winning at any of several different casino games. The slot section contains accurate, useful information, although I do disagree with a few of Steve's assumptions, such as the notion that you can tip an employee to tell you where hot slots are. They don't know—they *can't* know—that any machine is going to hit anywhere on the floor at any time, and I don't care how many times a machine *has* hit—it doesn't mean it's going to hit again tonight, or this week. He also suggests that one can tell when a slot is preparing to "dump" the contents of its hopper after it has not paid out for a long time. Contents of hoppers are monitored constantly and replenished daily, and have no relationship to the choice a slot computer's random number generator makes—and, with ticket-printing slots, the question is moot anyway.

One other suggestion that is only partly correct is that one can look at the mechanical coin-in and coin-out meters through the glass of a reel-spinning machine and calculate the payback percentage. The problem with this is that those meters do not tally hand-paid jackpots, which have a huge effect on overall payback percentage, and that, on many machines, the coin meters do not tally credit play, just actual coins inserted into the slot and dropping into the hopper. (Many newer games do not even have the meters, since most regulatory agencies have dropped the requirement they be included.)

But other than these few notions Gibbs's slot information is well-informed and quite valuable.

All of these products, in fact, offer many of the same tidbits of advice that I have sought to impart to you in this book, except without cornball lines or analogies containing the phrase "weasel manure."

And all of these books say right up front there's no way to guarantee you'll win at slots—that luck and the laws of randomness ultimately rule the day.

As for those "guaranteed" systems, don't waste your money. Save it to buy additional copies of this book. You won't be sorry.

(Neither will I.)

Chapter 8

Join
the Club

There are a few stories circulating through the casino world concerning how slot clubs were first formed. One story identifies the Golden Nugget in Atlantic City (which became Bally's Grand Casino Hotel, then the Grand Casino Hotel, and is now the Atlantic City Hilton Casino Hotel, and will some day be known simply as the White Place at the End of the Boardwalk Casino Hotel) as the site of the first slot club. Others insist that the Captain's Club at Harrah's Atlantic City (at the time known as Harrah's Marina) was the first slot club.

My personal theory is that slot clubs were created when Atlantic City casinos, through some sort of purchasing snafu, ended up with an inventory of, like, a trillion key chains.

SLOT MANAGER: Boss, what are we going to do with all these key chains?

BOSS: Let's give them away to customers. Let's see . . . we'll give them one key chain for every thousand dollars they put in the slots, until we unload all trillion key chains.

SLOT MANAGER : Great. Then, tomorrow, we'll give them something else.

For our purposes, the origin of the slot club doesn't really matter. They all do basically the same thing: they reward players for repeatedly plunking their hard-earned dollars into a given casino's slot machines.

Once people learned there was something called a slot club, of course, everyone *had* to join. That's because your average American will cheerfully eat all his meals from a dumpster if it means belonging to a "club." Belonging to a club means that, regardless of how much of a repugnant, vile, worm-eating beast you are personally, you belong to a "group" of people with interests that are similar to your own, and thus you fit in, in some ridiculous way, with one or more other humans.

In fact, as I noted once in a column, adult males possess a hormone that causes them to automatically join any club, just in case it meets in a treehouse. (I know, I know. No joke recycling. But that was a good one, don't you think?)

Once a member of a slot club, you will be surprised at the rewards you can generate for yourself simply by dropping every penny you possess into slot machines. No, seriously, you don't have to do that—you'll be amazed at how quickly points rack up in many casinos, even if you're winning. That's because the slot player tracking systems used by the casinos record money off the credit meter as "play," even if you end up with more money than when you started. It is true that a typical casino will take your final win/loss number for the session into account, but normally only as part of a complicated formula to determine your "theoretical worth" as a player—which means that you can win money on a slot machine and receive a cash coupon to boot, rewarding you for your play. You'll also get a variety of freebies from the casino if you play with reasonable frequency.

It wasn't always this way for slot players. Before the era of the slot club, casinos viewed slot players sort of the way an international opera star would view an audience full of drunken Mötley Crüe fans. They're here, so we'll take their money. By the mid-'80s, though, slot players were pumping millions into casinos. As the competition in Atlantic City heated up, slot managers (by that time professional executives, with job requirements beyond being the boss's brother-in-law) decided they had better treat these folks to some free stuff so they wouldn't go up the Boardwalk to the next casino. They figured slot players deserved to be treated like the table players.

So they gave them buffets and key chains.

This lasted a few years, until slot club members had bread pudding actually coming out of their ears, and enough key chains to hold a key to every lock on the North American continent. Restaurant comps got more high-class. The gifts got better: Clock radios. Sets of knives. Sets of forks. Casino-logo duffel bags. Casino-logo T-shirts. Casino-logo sweatshirts. Casino-logo underwear, brassieres, SCUBA-diving gear, clown suits, automatic rifles, and drug paraphernalia.

Finally, they got around to cash. People liked that. People still like that. Some casinos give you "same-day cash back" through the slot club—that means you can play the slots enough to earn cash back and get the money on the spot, in a few places even download-ing it right to your machine as credits. Others send out what they call "bounce-back" cash. This is a coupon that requires you to come back to the casino to get your money. Most have expiration dates, or spe-cific periods during which you must return to the casino if you want to redeem your cash coupon. Some require you to come on one spe-cific day to redeem it. Some require you to come on a specific day, at a specific time, dressed like Little Bo Peep, with your birth certificate, next of kin, blood and hair samples, results of a urine test, and proof that you have won the Congressional Medal of Honor to redeem your cash coupon.

Regardless of the redemption requirements, people love get-ting those cash coupons in the mail. Personally, I could mortgage my house, sell all my furniture, sell my dog, my cat, and my children, and blow all the money playing slots at a casino, and I'd still be excited when I got a $10 cash coupon in the mail that I'd earned from that slot play.

I know expert gamblers who use the cash-back system to the hilt, going on periodic "coupon runs" to collect hundreds of dollars worth of cash back at a clip. My friend Jean Scott, the "Queen of Comps," is like that. Jean could make a primary income out of cash back if she wanted to. Of course, Jean and her husband Brad retired from "real jobs" long ago and spend a good portion of their waking hours playing video poker, and writing articles and books about how to get the most from the comps available through slot clubs. They look for multiple-point days at local casinos, and build up big point totals to generate their cash back. Earning big chunks of cash back like that requires time. I, unfortunately, still have a real job (well, if you can call it that), so I'm still elated with the measly little $10 and $20 cash coupons. (I am truly pathetic.)

There are many gaming writers who rate the casinos by how generous their cash back is, figuring it down to fractional percentages of coin-in on each machine. I may know about slots, but I'm no expert on these fine points of minutia concerning slot clubs. I'll leave that sort of analysis to experts like Jeffrey Compton, another one of my gaming-writer pals. (Some day, we'll form a union. The International Amalgamated Brotherhood and Sisterhood of Gaming Writers, AFL/CIO, LS/MFT. We shall seize the means of production from the capitalist publishing bourgeois elite, and create the Dictatorship of the Gaming Writer Proletariat! Solidarity forever! Joe Hill! Attica! Attica! Living Room! Cellar!)

No, I'm not a slot club expert, nor do I play one on TV. However, because I'm based near Atlantic City, I have had all kinds of experience in another aspect of the slot clubs—promotions. The Atlantic City casinos are masters of the slot club promotion. Earn a few points, and you're sure to get invited to some sort of sweepstakes event, car giveaway, or slot tournament.

Sweepstakes events and car giveaways are pretty similar from casino to casino. You'll finally be winning on a slot game after losing all night, and an announcement will come over the PA system to go to a certain spot in the casino where an official in a business suit will pull entries out of a drum, or will hit a key on a computer to draw imaginary entries out of an imaginary drum. (If it's President's Day, the official will be dressed like Abe Lincoln. If it's Easter, he'll be in a rabbit suit. If it's Earth Day, he will be covered in dirt.) When you hear the sweepstakes announcement, you hit the "cash out" button on your slot, your hopper empties before you get your money, and you miss the entire drawing waiting for a fill. That's okay, though, because it's always the hundred-year-old woman from Peoria with no driver's license who wins the $100,000 Porsche Boxter sports car, and it's always the oil-rich Texas billionaire who wins the $50,000 in cash. The other winners get, like, a hundred dollars each, and half of them never wade through the crowd to claim their money, since they are still sitting at various locations in the casino waiting for hopper fills.

Slot tournaments also are pretty much the same from place to place, except for the different "themes" casinos use to promote them.

Casinos will buy "tournament chips" for a designated group of games. These designated machines will be set with payback percentages of, say, 150 percent, so jackpots hit left and right. The machines will be loaded with an initial amount of credits, and the people with the most credits on their machines at the end of the tournament session get the highest scores, and win a set amount of money according to their place in the scoring.

In practice, it goes like this: Say you're invited to a Valentine's Day slot tournament. The casino will invite you in for two free nights, during which you will gamble away your entire net worth. Once or twice during your trip, you will be assigned to go into a room decked out in Valentine's hearts with a group of other players and bang furiously for 10 minutes on the "spin" button of a video slot. Then, you get dinner and maybe win back a portion of your former net worth. (If it's a New Year's Eve slot tournament, you'll get a funny hat and a party horn, and the room will be decked out in party ribbons. If it's the Fourth of July, the room will be red, white, and blue, and the casino officials will be dressed like Uncle Sam.)

If this were all you got in the way of slot club promotions, one would think the casino marketing departments had little creativity. But sweepstakes and tournaments are just the promotions that everyone does. More and more, particularly in Atlantic City, you will find lots of wacky, inventive stuff as well. The Tropicana periodically employs a bunch of live chickens—yes, actual, breathing, clucking, feathered birds—which play tic-tac-toe games with slot club members. And almost always win. When the promotion's on, they keep around 15 of the chickens at the hotel. Presumably, they are comped, and are lodged in the hotel's Chicken Wing. (Nyuk!)

But, anyway, every slot club member gets one chance per day to beat a chicken at tic-tac-toe. They put one of the little peckers in a see-through box, and the chicken gets the first move. The chicken pecks at something inside that you can't see, an "X" appears on a tic-tac-toe board, the player makes his move, and the game continues. If you win the game, the Trop pays you $10,000. If the chicken wins, he earns one more day of living large in a hotel, ordering chicken room service ("Feed Flambeau"), exercising on chicken treadmills in the Chicken Spa, swimming in the Chicken Pool, sending chicken dinners to his chicken buddy's room as a practical joke, and pursuing whatever other recreation chickens pursue.

If you are reasonably proficient at tic-tac-toe (definition: "anyone other than me"), it is likely the match will end in a tie. The chicken wins the push. (Isn't that always the way?)

Believe it or not, this is no con job. The chickens do lose occasionally. The Trop has awarded a bunch of $10,000 prizes already, after players have beaten the birds at their own game. One would think the losers end up on the dinner menu, but they don't. I researched it. I asked their trainer (yes, a professional chicken trainer), Bunky Boger (yes, "Bunky Boger"), what happens to the chickens who lose, and he said they are just taken out of the regular chicken rotation for a while and given time to regain their chicken composure. In other words, they're benched for a period before being returned to the pecking order. They let them simmer for a while. I guess they grill them on the rules. So they don't commit another fowl. (Okay, I'll stop.)

Harrah's is another casino known for fun promotions. A few years ago, they had one called the Dig in the Desert. Slot club members at Harrah's casinos around the country participated in preliminary drawings, and the winners were all flown to Las Vegas, where they were given treasure maps. They were then all assigned to SUVs and taken out into the desert, where they were killed.

No, seriously, they were taken out into the desert to hunt for buried treasure. Aided by guides, they each found a treasure chest containing a cash prize. One of the cash prizes was the top one—a cool million bucks. I think a wealthy Texas oil billionaire won it.

Sometimes, casinos make their slot club sweepstakes into game shows. Harrah's used the Game of LIFE as the basis for a promotion a few years ago. All the preliminary drawings used the famous board game to devise clever little events, with titles such as "How Pathetic Is My LIFE?"

And then there's the "Bally Bowl." Every year during football season, slot club members at Bally's Atlantic City pick the winners of each week's NFL games. The players with the most correct picks win big piles of cash. Personally, I set a record in this promotion, for which I always thought I should have gotten some sort of recognition. I believe I am the only slot club member ever to have gotten every single pick wrong. The players who won simply looked at my card and picked the opposite teams.

Casinos usually tie their promotions to whatever greeting cards are available at a given time of year. A few years ago on Valentine's Day, at the Taj Mahal in Atlantic City, "Cupid" ran around the casino "shooting" random slot players with his "arrow of love" to designate them for cash prizes. Of course, the casino had no promotion going that day. Fortunately, only a few players were injured before Cupid was wrestled to the ground by security guards.

There also are a lot of promotions designed strictly to get you to join the slot club, usually with promises of multiple points, an initial cash coupon, or, occasionally, something more enticing. A few years ago, Caesars came up with one that let new members guess an eight-digit number. If it was the same eight-digit number that the casino had locked in a vault somewhere, you won a million dollars on the spot. Of course, the odds were better that one million purple ducks would fly down from the sky and each give you a dollar.

I have periodically suggested in columns that I can come up with my own clever slot club promotions. But the casinos never seem to agree. Not one of them, for instance, picked up on my suggestion for a slot-club "Senior Boxing" competition. My "Pull-My-Finger Bean Dinner and Slot Tournament" never materialized either. And I got nowhere with my suggestion that slot club members be given the opportunity to wager on a contest between Donald Trump and Steve Wynn, in which the casino moguls would fight to the death.

Besides the promotions and merchandise gifts, casinos are always giving their slot club members free rooms and free show tickets. You normally do not have to play a whole lot to get invited in for a free room night and two tickets to a performance in which someone who was a TV star 30 years ago will sing, dance, or tell jokes. I receive cards every week offering me free tickets to, say, "The Charles Nelson Reilly Show" or "The Charo/Jimmy Walker 'Dy-no-mite!' Revue," or maybe the "Slappy White Retrospective."

The Tropicana in Atlantic City will also invite slot club members to all of these educational touring exhibits they bring into their ballrooms. A few years ago, they brought in artifacts from the wreck of the *Titanic*. They also had an exhibit of John F. Kennedy memorabilia, including things like personal notes from Jack to Jackie, or from Jack to Bobby, or from Jack to Sam Giancana. Another one was "Torture Through the Ages," an exhibit of instruments of torture ranging from the rack and the iron maiden to the complete library of the television show *One Day at a Time*.

My wife's favorite was an exhibit that basically consisted of a roomful of dresses that had been worn by Princess Diana. It was called "Dresses of Diana, Princess of Wales." (The Trop declined my offer to put together a follow-up exhibit called "Overalls of Ralph, Mechanic of Scranton.")

In any event, my point in noting all these benefits of slot club membership, besides getting some cheap laughs at the expense of my favorite casinos, is that it is just plain dumb to play slots without first inserting your slot club card. Otherwise, when you lose, you're just giving your money to the casino without getting anything in return.

Besides, if you don't use your card, where are you going to get your key chains?

Chapter 9

Is That Popeye or Mammy Yokem?

Back in the early days of the slot machine, a "theme" meant one thing: three reels, fruit and bar symbols, and 7s. The only differences among themes were the different colors of the fruit, bar symbols, and 7s, the design on the slot glass, and the name.

That was, of course, BWOF. That is to say, Before *Wheel of Fortune*. Once IGT started raking in the loot with that game, all the manufacturers began using clever themes for their games. Some used TV shows. Some used board games. Some used movies. Some used Elvis. Some used little cartoon pigs that looked like Elvis.

The point was to entertain. By the mid-1990s, the playing public had, remarkably, become a little tired of watching reels spin around. (Imagine that.) People wanted more entertainment. In fact, they were starved for entertainment (at least outside of the political arena). That's why Anchor Games was able to do things like attaching a drainpipe to the top of a slot machine and make millions in profit. Regular bonus features like multiplying wild symbols were no longer enough for everyone. The slot-makers would fill the void with themes.

When playing themed games, remember what I told you in that other chapter—the funny cartoons are there to make you laugh your head off while you cheerfully lose money. Make sure the bonus sequences happen often enough that you don't have to keep feeding the machine to pay for the cartoons. The cartoons sometimes perform the function of diverting you from the fact that your overall session is a losing one. They are there to replenish your credit meter temporarily and to be so entertaining that you'll want to dip into your wallet to see it again. They are there to . . . yadda yadda yadda, blah blah blah. Never mind all that stuff, because these games are fun. And there are so many different themes out there, covering just about everything you have ever seen in your life, that you have plenty of options from which to choose.

At first, most of the themes used to promote slot machines to the public were proprietary creations of the slot machine manufacturers. "Piggy Bankin'" from WMS Gaming allowed the player to collect bonus money in a piggy bank displayed on an LED screen; when a certain symbol hit on the reels, the bank would break, and the LED display would show the pig go into a dance, or sprout sideburns and change into Pig-Elvis and say "Thangya. Thangyaverymuch." Reel 'Em In, also from WMS, was the first American-themed multi-line video slot, featuring a cartoon in which politically correct fisherpersons with Chicago accents cast their lines for bonus money. It was accompanied by a similar game called Filthy Rich, with its cartoon in which a farmer hoses off his pigs to reveal bonus amounts. (WMS has sort of a thing for pigs.)

IGT, though, quickly became the King of Themes. By the late 1990s, the manufacturer was sitting comfortably atop the slot market, with enough profit to purchase anything it wanted, including, say, Canada or Argentina. (Had I bought a few shares of IGT when I got into this racket in the mid-'80s, I would not be writing this book. I would be on my own island somewhere working on my tan. Another example of my astute knack for market analysis.) But, instead of buying countries, IGT bought licenses to use icons of popular culture as themes for new slot games.

One of the biggies early on was "Elvis," a reel-spinning game with a multisite progressive jackpot that included a bonus game displaying the King of Rock and Roll performing one of his songs. The video clips were taken from Elvis Presley performance footage such as his 1968 "comeback" TV special, or his 1973 "Aloha from Hawaii" concert, so they all showed Elvis in his prime, belting out tunes in top form, his still-thin body decked out in leather or in one of those sequin-studded jumpsuits when they still actually fit him. A sequel slot game called Elvis Hits offered more of the same from the King when he still looked like a Greek god (assuming that Greek gods soaked their hair in enough black dye to blot out the sun).

Those two Elvis games are still out there in a lot of casinos, and we're all still waiting for the next sequel: "Elvis—Peanut Butter and Preludin." It will feature concert footage of Elvis in his final years, mumbling incoherently on stage and wearing jumpsuits which each required enough material to make three circus tents.

Anyway, Elvis was one of the first of many high-profile licenses IGT would purchase, and it would start a trend for the company's MegaJackpots games. MegaJackpots is the name the company gave to its series of big-money progressive slots that started when Rich Little introduced Megabucks to my nauseated, hung-over self in 1986. By the mid-'90s, the company had done every conceivable alteration to slots called Megabucks—there was a four-reel Megabucks, a three-reel Megabucks, dollar Megabucks, Megabucks Quartermania, Megabucks Nevada Nickels, Megabucks Schenectady Half-Dollars, and on and on. Beginning with *Wheel of Fortune*, a Megabucks-style jackpot created through a portion of coins wagered at every machine on a statewide network became a staple of any number of games bearing familiar themes.

After the Elvis slot was introduced to players—often with a big "first-pull" ceremony hosted by a fat guy in an Elvis suit—IGT decided to go back to the game-show well with *Jeopardy!* (It's not that I'm excited this transpired. The exclamation point is in the title itself.) This was basically Megabucks with a picture of Alex Trebek and a bonus game that showed the big board from the game show—only where the game show has dollar amounts for different questions in various categories, the slot game had bonus coin awards. ("I'll take 'My Son's College Fund' for a hundred dollars, Alex.")

Alex himself—whose real name is "Alec," because he's Canadian—was on hand at Showboat Atlantic City for the Ceremonial First Pull of the *Jeopardy!* game. Before he did it, he proclaimed, "I feel lucky!" and proceeded to pull a losing spin. He was determined to pull that handle until a winning combination came up, so he kept feeding dollars into the slot and feeling lucky until, with sweat beading on his embarrassed forehead, he finally scored a two-coin hit on the Ceremonial Four Thousandth Pull.

Players went wacky for *Jeopardy!* anyway, because, as I explained in a previous chapter, it had TV stuff. One annoying thing it also had, though, occurred when the bonus round was triggered—a sound-bite blared from the speakers: "This. Is. *Jeopardy!*" The first time you heard this while playing a nearby slot, you said to yourself, "Gee, isn't that clever? Just like the announcer on the TV show!" The twelve millionth time you heard it—if the bank of games was busy, you'd hear three or four announcers saying "This is *Jeopardy!*" at once—you were quivering on the brink of insanity, battling an urge to go get a machine gun. ("*I'll* show him what *jeopardy* is, by God!")

There were a few more early themed games that gained success as reel-spinners—WMS Gaming came out with Jackpot Party during this period. This game is still wildly popular today and was a pioneering slot for the manufacturer, in that it did not include a fish or a pig.

But the real party for the themed game started in video. After advancements in computer technology permitted video cartoon animation or even live-action video to be loaded into slot games and displayed to the player with the quality of a home video game, the slot-makers all began to snatch up licenses to create games based on TV cartoons, TV game shows, TV sitcoms, TV commercials, movies, movie cartoons, movie stars, cartoon movie stars, board games, magazines, puzzles, comic books, comic strips, hot sauce, 1960s fads, 1970s fads, luncheon meat, and anything else they could find from scouring through the grimy, vermin-infested, stench-emitting corners of American popular culture.

As I explained earlier, all of these games operate in basically the same manner as the modern reel-spinners: they are computers that run through numbers in a program and pick one when the spin is initiated. But they all have a bonus game added when a certain number is picked. The player's award will be random for that game, but the way it is displayed is the product of video animators. Instead of picking one of five rocks to find a buried bonus "treasure," you'll pick, say, one of Popeye's barnacles, or one of the liver spots on Bowzer from Sha Na Na.

The period from 1999 through today can accurately be described as the "Golden Age of the Slot Theme." When I thought up that title (and I have it trademarked, so don't get any ideas), I decided to search through my archives for a few examples of themes from different slot manufacturers that have appeared since 1999. It is part of the extensive research on which you can count when reading this book. In this instance, it involved me staring at the wall of my office and performing an exercise which, in the professional journalism business, is technically described as "thinking."

I began to jot down a few slot themes that have come out in the past couple of years. I am now on my 10th page of themes: Addams Family. Munsters. Marilyn Monroe. Frank Sinatra. The Beverly Hillbillies. Popeye. Pac-Man. Ray Charles. Mr. Magoo. Playboy. Spider-Man. Beetle Bailey. Bewitched. Betty Boop. Monopoly. Trivial Pursuit. Ripley's Believe It or Not! The Honeymooners. I Love Lucy. I Love Ricky. I Love Fred and Ethel. The Three Stooges. Wink Martindale. Miss America. "Wink Martindale, Miss America." Frankie and Annette. Laurel and Hardy. Conway and Korman. Sacco and Vanzetti.

Evel Knievel. Yahtzee. Battleship. The Price Is Right. Blondie. Kenny Rogers. Hollywood Squares. Hollywood Rectangles. Survivor. Clue. Rubik's Cube. Winning for Dummies. Budweiser. Andy Capp. Richard Petty's Driving Experience. Press Your Luck. I Dream of Jeannie. I Dream of Marvin.

Suddenly, most of the companies in the slot-making universe were competing for licenses to make the next big slot game. IGT signed a deal to make a *Newlywed Game* slot, and Bally quickly snatched up Bob Eubanks, the longtime host, to do another slot. So now players can see Bob Eubanks hosting Cash for Life by Bally, and can see a *Newlywed Game* by IGT, hosted by Jim Lange. I thought the host would be Larry King. Or maybe Don King.

Silicon Gaming, a slot manufacturer that, in 1996, had created a space-age slot machine called Odyssey that had breathtaking 3-D graphics and looked like a personal computer and was actually played by about six people, snatched up licenses to create slots based on the game shows *Family Feud* and *The Price Is Right*. Silicon released a *Family Feud* game that had all kinds of neat stuff, like a camera that took the slot player's picture and placed him in the video bonus round as a contestant. MGM Grand created a dedicated area for the game, decked out like the *Feud* set. (Players, though, fled the area in a horrified frenzy once they saw the life-size cutout of host Louie

Anderson.) IGT officials wanted both of those licenses to create *Family Feud* and *Price Is Right* games of their own. They couldn't buy the licenses, so they just bought Silicon Gaming. (IGT motto: "We Own You, or We Will.")

IGT, meanwhile, set out to prove it can take anything in the world that has a trademark and make a slot game out of it. "Tabasco": the first slot game in history to display all the gambling nuances of a popular condiment. (Next up: "Soy Sauce.") "SPAM": The king of slot machines meets the gunnery sergeant of luncheon meat.

Licensed themes are still proliferating like conservative talk-radio hosts, but there are also hundreds of slot themes out there that required no license. The slot manufacturers have accompanied the branded theme boom with a boom of proprietary, right-out-of-their-sick-minds slot themes.

Some of these themes have been cute. Some have been a little wacky. Some have led to speculation that product development staffs at slot manufacturers are required to include at least one escaped mental patient who never takes his medication.

One of the earliest—and still one of the most popular—proprietary themes was IGT's Little Green Men. It has a cartoon bonus round in which you get to pick one of several regular shmoes sitting at a bus stop to be abducted by aliens. As he is beamed up to the spaceship, a bonus amount appears in his spot—apparently, it is the amount left by the aliens to compensate the guy's family for having abducted him.

Bally countered with a game called Cash Encounters, which also has an alien-abduction theme. Only in this bonus round the spaceship beams up a bunch of cows that were grazing in a field. This game marked what was perhaps the first time in history that people sitting in a casino, surrounded by the glitz and glitter of Vegas gaming, could honestly say they heard several cows say "moo."

There has been lots of this kind of one-upmanship by the slot manufacturers when it comes to themes. For instance, there are now three different games from three different slot-makers that show cartoon strip-tease routines. It all started when Aristocrat mined the slightly askew brains of its Australian idea-men to come up with Keep Your Hat On, which has a hilarious cartoon bonus sequence of a male stripper grinning and mugging for the camera as he takes off everything but his hat, which spins around right over his whatchamacallit. Atronic, a slot-maker whose slightly askew idea-men are Austrian, countered with Chickendales, which has a bonus round featuring blubbery, overweight cartoon chickens, who do not have whatchamacallits, doing a strip-tease dance. Not to be outdone, IGT released Risqué Business, the first video slot to feature a politically correct strip-tease dance—the player gets to choose whether the cartoon strippers will be male or female, proving once and for all that off-color gaming entertainment is gender-neutral, and is available to all regardless of sexual preference. God bless America!

Not that anyone has to copy themes; there are plenty to go around. Atronic has everything from its Sphinx series, which takes the player on a 3-D trip through a pharaoh's tomb, to Crazy Fruits, with crated fruits speaking in a weird, slightly disturbing voice. (This game apparently targets schizophrenics.) Bally has everything from video versions of Blazing 7s to irreverent stuff like Pearly Gates, which features the Hand of God and bonus awards granted according to whether apparently dead cartoon characters sprout wings and fly to Heaven or are zapped by the Big Guy's lightning and have their damned souls drop toward the fiery bowels of Gehenna.

Some themes have even created controversy. The Political Correctness Police had a few concerns over IGT's Fortune Cookie, which features a hysterical shameless stereotype of a Chinese chef talking in a comical accent about items on his menu. IGT, of course, maintained that the fact its game's main character acted like Hop-Sing on *Bonanza* was purely coincidental, and that it "regletted any offense taken over our new srot machine."

(Not to be outdone in animated depictions of comical foreigners, Sigma Game released a slot called Throw the Dough, featuring "Luigi," a fat, mustachioed "goombah" in a chef hat twirling pizza and talking in a hilarious, stereotypical Italian accent.)

Then there was the ridiculous "Slots for Tots" controversy, in which Nevada regulators began refusing to approve slot themes that appeared to appeal to children, who are not allowed in casinos. They refused to approve IGT's *South Park*, because it is based on a cartoon, even though the cartoon on which it is based—which features foul-mouthed little kids—is on cable late at night and is targeted toward adults. (Popeye, based on a cartoon directed primarily at children that involves fun-filled physical abuse, was apparently okay.)

Then, the Nevada *regulatóres* made the former CDS Gaming alter the graphics on the screen of the slot game Easy Street, because they said the bonus game board resembled the children's game Candy Land. Okay, the thing looked *exactly* like Candy Land. My little girl wanted to play it. But the point is, she isn't allowed to go into casinos. (Not until she's old enough to use a fake ID.)

But, anyway, with all the controversy over slots that may appeal to children, I was forced to scrap some of my own slot theme ideas, which included games like "Big Bird's Bonus Bonanza," "Mister Rogers' Casino," and "Barney Goes to the Track."

I wasn't concerned that I had to scrap a few slot ideas. The manufacturers have always known they could count on me for a continuous stream of demented ideas on stuff that would make great slot themes. I'm sure some of them read my columns just to draw theme ideas.

I think up new slot theme ideas all the time. As a matter of fact, I am going to share some of them with you right now, in an entire chapter dedicated to the slot themes we would like to see.

First, a note to the slot manufacturers: Any themes I suggest in the following pages are available to you by simply sending me a big pile of cash. I'll give you my home address. Send me money. Right now. (Okay, at least buy the book. Quit reading it in the bookstore. What, you think this is a library?)

Chapter 10

Theme
This

Right about the time all the slot manufacturers began creating all these fun themes in which to cloak their slot bonus games, I began writing humor columns about casinos. It started with the editor's letter I used to write for the late, great *Atlantic City Insider* newsletter. For a month in which sister publication *Casino Player* published its annual "Best of Gaming" feature, which included solemn descriptions of why this or that casino feature was voted by readers to be the best in the business, I decided things were getting too serious and did a spoof called "Top Ten Things Missed by Best of Gaming." I gave Tropicana the award for Best Place to Panhandle, and Donald Trump the award for Best Example of Shameless Self-Promotion by a Chief Executive.

After that, I started doing funny columns now and then, and eventually every month. Everyone seemed to like it—even the people in the industry whom I busted on constantly. (Let me take this opportunity to pause and once again thank the former executives of the Claridge for being such great sports about me saying things like, the average player age at the hotel was one hundred, or noting that the hotel opened in 1930, when most of its current customers were middle-aged.) When we started *Strictly Slots* at the end of 1998, my boss asked me to do a humor column in the back of the book, which became "Perfectly Frank."

With slot manufacturers creating goofy themes and me doing goofy columns, it was inevitable that I would soon begin spewing ideas for my own goofy slot themes. I've built up my own library of slot themes I'd like to see. I have pursued no licenses for these ideas, because I don't have the tools needed for such pursuits, like money. I have not offered to partner with any slot manufacturers to develop these ideas into slot games, because I lack certain key necessities of such partnerships, such as money. By giving them to you right now, free of charge, I am baring my soul and placing my own brain drippings on public display for the benefit of all, in the hope that, on some ethereal plane or by benefit of my own selfless giving, I will gain certain intangible rewards. Such as money.

My personal game library is divided into categories, and I've already written marketing copy for each game.

I'll start out with my personal "TV Category." The real slot manufacturers have certainly done their best to mine the rich vein of television situation comedy from the 1950s and 1960s, but there are many shows they have missed. For instance:

Mayberry RNG. Welcome back to that sleepy North Carolina town of Mayberry, where Sheriff Taylor has just signed an agreement with Harrah's to build a casino out at the old fishin' pond. The player wins a bonus every time Barney Fife quits fishing long enough to crack another roll of quarters.

My Mother the Slot. In this wacky bonus game Jerry Van Dyke is back as Dave, the hapless husband who discovers his mother has come back from the dead as a slot machine. See Dave go through a hilarious philosophical crisis when faced with having to pull his mother's handle, and reach the top bonus level, which features a madcap animated sequence in which Dave beats another player up for pounding on his mother to summon a jackpot.

Batman. No joke here. It would just be a really cool game.

Green Acres. I'm surprised no one has come up with this one yet (although there is a video slot that uses the theme song). Basically, the bonus rounds would make no changes from the actual show, which evidently was written by comedians on LSD. The game would, however, dispense drugs to the player prior to the bonus round.

One TV theme I created in a column once is now an actual slot machine. It wasn't that someone took my idea, but they apparently got the same notion around the same time I did. I wrote in a column about an imaginary *Newlywed Game* slot in which animated husbands were bludgeoned to death by their animated wives after an insensitive answer, using an animated blunt object. When the column was published, I got a call from a guy at IGT who said their *Newlywed Game*, still in development at the time, has a bonus round in which basically the same thing happens. Oh, well. Great minds think alike.

Some slot-makers have graduated from TV to movie themes, so I've done the same thing. In my personal "Movie Theme" slot category, I have a few games that could some day be your favorites:

The Godfather. Those wacky Sicilians are back, in a veritable *Cosa Nostra* of bonus fun! Collect bonus credits for every hole in Sonny Corleone's bullet-riddled corpse! Get to the main bonus round and collect big rewards as the head of each of the five families gets "whacked" by Michael Corleone's goons! It's a bonus offer you can't refuse!

The Good, the Bad, and Clint Eastwood. This game has a multi-level bonus round in which Clint Eastwood's lonely cowboy drifter character from the spaghetti Westerns takes on every subsequent Clint Eastwood character. The drifter rides into the South and shoots Josey Wales, then rides to Carmel, Calif., to shoot Mayor Eastwood, and finally ends up in San Francisco, where he is shot by Dirty Harry, and then propped up and shot again by Dirty Harry. The player must then guess whether or not Dirty Harry has another bullet in his gun, as Eastwood invites the player to ask himself, "'Do I feel lucky?' Well, *do ya, punk?"*

Dances with Wolves. This game has a bonus round in which the player has to guess just how much of a laboriously long movie Kevin Costner is capable of making, and how many hours will pass before you are ready to rip up the screen. If the player makes all the right selections and the movie reaches four hours, he goes into a second-level bonus—"Waterworld." That round takes about three weeks to finish.

Like the slot manufacturers, I have not forgotten that fabulously successful slot games can emerge merely from the image of a celebrity. In my personal "Celebrity Theme" category, my favorite is the *Henny Youngman* video slot. A triggering combination on the video reels transforms the screen into an image of the "King of the One Liners" in the Catskills, in black tie, drink in one hand, microphone in the other. The bonus game would be called "Finish the Joke." Henny gives the setup, and the player has to pick the right punch line:

HENNY: Psychiatrist's nurse says, "Doctor, there's a man in the waiting room who says he's invisible." Doctor says . . .
TOP BONUS PUNCH LINE: "Tell him I can't see him."

HENNY: Doctor gave a man six months to live. Couldn't pay his bill.
TOP BONUS PUNCH LINE: He gave him another six months.

HENNY: My wife and I were happy for 20 years.
TOP BONUS PUNCH LINE: Then we met.

Well, you get the idea. (And, yes, you are correct. The preceding theme was simply a pretense to squeeze some corny one-liners into the book.)

A couple other celebrity themes from my library:

Anna Nicole. A fanciful bonus flight through Anna Nicole Smith's day, in which the player follows Anna Nicole from pizza parlor to burger joint to hot dog stand. In the main bonus, the player is shown an animated image of Anna Nicole and live-action video from her reality show, and asked to pick which most resembles a cartoon.

NRA. I've included this in the Celebrity Theme category because it would feature Charlton Heston. I actually wrote about this one in *Strictly Slots,* prompting one gun-enthusiast reader to write a letter calling me a pinko commie left-winger. It is for this reason I revive it here.

Basically, the video slot would feature former NRA president Charlton Heston, and reel symbols such as AK-47s, M-16s, and Glock 9 mm semiautomatics. In the bonus round, Charlton Heston morphs into Moses and distributes firearms to the Israelites.

(It is a *joke,* all you gun enthusiasts. Ha-ha! It doesn't mean I'm a pinko commie left-winger. It doesn't mean anything. Please don't shoot me.)

Finally, in the "Proprietary Theme" category (Frank Legato, Prop., Est. March 2003), I have several slot themes for which I don' need no stinkin' license:

All In. Play the first slot machine able to tap directly into your private bank accounts and credit lines! Various bonus levels let you bet your bank balances, stocks and bonds, trust funds, real estate properties—the whole enchilada! Go "all in" in a head-to-head poker match with an animated banker! Think of it. Two results: Instant wealth beyond your imagination, or a future of living in an appliance carton under a bridge. What an adrenaline rush! Scout some good manhole-cover locations before you play, and don't forget to bring your wife's account numbers!

Pot-Head. Relive those adolescent days you spent wandering about in a marijuana haze! Three or more "fried brain cell" symbols on an active payline trigger the "Pink Floyd Bonus." Sit in semicomatose, drooling wonder as the sound system plays the entire *Dark Side of the Moon* album. Don't forget the Twinkies!

The Man Game. Play the slot that's made by guys, for guys! Progress to one of the manly bonus rounds to pick the answer to a wifely question. The right answer gets a bonus. The wrong answer ends the bonus round as you are clubbed beyond recognition by your cartoon spouse. For example, the player is shown the question, "Does this dress make me look fat?"

CORRECT BONUS ANSWER: That's impossible, darling.
WRONG BONUS ANSWER: Not if you're Marlon Brando.

The main bonus round follows a beer-gutted guy through his ideal daily routine: Get up at 11 o'clock. Open beer. Watch sports while opening beers. Watch *Celebrity Female Porn Star Mud Wrestling* while opening beers. Have sex with the participants of *Celebrity Female Porn Star Mud Wrestling* while opening beers. Take a break to have a beer. Take another break to defend yourself to your significant other for an insensitive remark you made in 1978, while opening beers. Go to bed and sleep for three days, taking periodic beer breaks.

What a Nimrod. This game combines every annoying, repulsive characteristic of every idiot you have ever encountered on the floor of a casino and combines them into an interactive bonus game in which the player uses a joystick to go on an animated, psychotic shooting spree to wipe out composite "jerkweed" characters.

I can't give you any details on the characters used in this game, though, because as it happens they are the very characters detailed in our next chapter. So on we go.

But first, a final word on themes:

HENNY: My wife likes to talk during sex.
TOP BONUS PUNCH LINE: Last week she called me from a motel.

(Sorry. I couldn't resist.)

Chapter 11

Who Was That Jerk? Oh, It Was Me

Well, dear readers, it is time to turn from our discussion of the innards and the outtards, the dos and the don'ts, the yins and the yangs, the Freds and the Barneys of the slot machine itself, and have a peek into the flotsam and jetsam of society that make up the humans and sub-creatures who provide the living, breathing element of the modern slot floor.

Damn. Was that a kick-ass sentence, or what?

Yes, in the following chapters, we will examine the nature of those individuals who surround slot machines in whatcha call yer "modern American world." We will also examine their environs, the casinos themselves, and the cultures that have built up surrounding each casino, each joint, each honky-tonk, each gin mill in each of several casino jurisdictions around the country, as we go "on the road with Frankie" to casinos East, West, South, North, and North by Northwest. Starting with the next chapter, we will all pack up our "gear," stuff our suitcases with clothes, grab the gas masks and nerve gas antidotes, and "hit the road" for some serious "gaming entertainment."

But, before we hit the road, you must be educated—indeed, *cautioned*—regarding many of the types of people we will find out on the casino road. Oh, don't worry. The vast majority of your encounters will be with normal, fun-loving, happy-go-lucky Middle Americans, who are just like you, except for the fact they are someone else. But there is a particular strain of proto-person that will occasionally rear its vile head as you are strutting merrily about the casino wearing your hippest fanny pack. They belong to a species known as *Slotticus jerkus,* or, in its formal English translation, "Nitwit Jerks You Just Want to Punch."

I have separated the members of the *Slotticus jerkus* species into specific categories. I will leave it to the encyclopedias to order these subspecies in logical progression according to significance, or even alphabetically. These are in no particular order, because that would involve effort.

Machine Whackers
(Slotticus jerkus abusus)

This strain of jerk seems to view the computerized slot machine in front of him as some sort of evil, cowardly entity who can be pounded into submission through physical abuse. Upon losing repeatedly, he will begin to punch the console between spins. Often, this action is accompanied by an exclamation which cannot be repeated in a family book such as this (that's right—buy one for each member of your family!), but which can be clinically described as calling the machine "one who performs a biological function necessary for reproduction with one's maternal parent."

These cretins will spin, and then punch, and say, "You person who performs a biological function with a maternal parent, you!" and spin again, and punch again, and say, "You person who uses your mouth to perform a vacuum action on a bodily part described by the one-syllable word for a rooster, you!" and so on.

Sometimes they'll slap the console; sometimes they'll punch it. But there is a constant stream of these two particular terms. You must have guessed what these are by now. *Don't make me spell them out!*

I have four words for all you Machine Whackers out there: *It's a friggin' machine!* You moron! (Okay, so I added two more.) When you hit it, punch it, or kick it, it does not say "Ouch!" and reevaluate its game plan in light of your violent reaction. It doesn't think to itself, "That *hurts,* man! I'd better start dishing out some jackpots before this nut-ball jars something loose inside of me!" It doesn't think at all. It has no cognitive reasoning capability. It is a mechanism. There is no entity inside. If there was, its fellow entities would surely rise up against you and stuff your sorry ass inside the gears of the Big Bertha slot at the end of the aisle. Because that's exactly what I'm thinking about doing after sitting beside you for two minutes.

Smoke-Free Crusaders
(Slotticus jerkus Everett Koopicus)

All right, it's not something of which I am particularly proud—I am a smoker. But I only smoke when I drink and gamble. (Of course, I drink and gamble constantly.) There are more and more "smoke-free casinos" these days. Now, when I go into one of these places, I do not sit next to nonsmokers and start complaining bitterly that I'm not allowed to light up. Yet, when nonsmokers come into a smoking casino, and invariably sit down *right next to me* even if I'm the only player in a bank of machines, they start in on me almost immediately.

Some ask me politely if I would put my cigarette out, and I always do. As Brando said in *The Godfather,* I'm a reasonable man. If a reasonable request is thrown my way, a reasonable, accommodating reaction is assured. But *Slotticus jerkus Everett Koopicus* nonsmoking players do not think of such a logical, rational course of action, because their problem is not that they want me to put this particular cigarette out. They want to snuff *me* out, personally—along with every other piece of dirt who may get the outrageous notion that one may burn tobacco in the presence of another human. These folks are all members of a group, which I identified in a *Strictly Slots* column a few years ago, called the Anti-Smoking Crusaders from Hell (ASCH).

First, the "Crusader" will try to shame me into not smoking through nonverbal cues. Basically, he will wave his hand like a fan and scrunch his face into a hideous contortion at the same time, until he looks like a circus freak waving bye-bye.

If this doesn't work, then the inevitable scare tactics begin, in the form of public health bulletins:

"You know, that's bad for you."

Really? I never heard that before! You see, I've been cryogenically frozen since 1963.

"You know, my cousin died from smoking when he was 57."

Great! Now he doesn't have to worry about Social Security drying up.

"I quit smoking because my wife wanted me to be around for a while."

Well, tell your wife to speak for herself.

"Why don't you quit? You'll feel better."

Why don't you leave? I'll feel a lot better sooner.

It's not that I want to smoke for the rest of my life. I've already quit twice this year, and I figure that next time it will stick. (First, I've got to finish writing this book, an activity which requires me to wear a fedora with a "PRESS" card in the band, with loosened tie and rolled up sleeves, and a lit cigarette dangling out of the side of my mouth. And a bottle of bourbon in the desk drawer. I can't help it. It's the law.) It's just that I don't really need others to tell me smoking is bad for me, and, knowing as I do that nonsmokers have the option to not sit down right next to me, I'd like to be cut a little slack for now, okay?

I'll quit. I promise. Just not right now. Got it?

So for now, Mr. Crusader, when you tell me that "most heart attacks are caused by smoking," I will always give you the same response:

"Hey, cardiologists gotta eat too, don't they?"

Machine Hogs
(Slotticus jerkus swinicus)

We've all seen them. They stake out not one, not two, but three, even four machines. Normally, they do not possess a rear end large enough to straddle four slot stools (although some certainly come close). However, they will put player's club cards in all four machines and throw some coins in each slot. Then, they'll sit down at one machine and play, periodically getting up to throw a coin in one of the other three.

Okay, a little quirky maybe, but it doesn't make them jerks. It is only when the credit meter on one of "their" four machines is at zero, and another player has the unmitigated gall to sit down to play it, that a Machine Hog instantly morphs into a jerk, a wiener, a boorish clod . . . what we used to refer to back in Pittsburgh as a *jag-off*.

"*Hey, that's mmmyyyy machine!*"

"But you're not playing it," you will say.

"I have it *reserved!* I'm playing all of them!"

What is incredible in this situation is that the casino will usually back the putz up, especially if he's a "good player." They figure it's good to have four machines that are guaranteed to be played by someone who bets a lot, even if he is a pinhead. So they will protect the Machine Hog's "turf," which he himself has been guarding like a hungry boar guarding his kill.

Oh, and don't be mistaken—Machine Hogs come in both sexes. The only difference is that, when one violates the female Machine Hog's turf, one will hear "That's *mmmyyyy* machine!" in a much more shrill voice.

If you run into this situation with a male Machine Hog, though, my advice is always the same: Ask the man in a polite, accommodating way if he is playing the game that is four machines removed from him. If he says, "Yeah, that's *my* machine," just politely say, "No problem—I'll find another game, sir. Have a nice day." Then, kick him in the groin.

Chit-Chatters
(Slotticus jerkus diarrhea mouthicus)

Now, I don't want to seem stand-offish or anything, but, when I play slots or video poker —especially video poker—human interaction is not necessarily something I seek (except, of course, from the cocktail waitress). I like to form a cocoon around myself so it's just me and the evil, vengeful entity of a computer, locked in a battle that will only be won if I punch the entity's lights out.

Yes, I can "chat" with someone a bit when I'm playing a regular slot. But, when I'm playing video poker, a modicum of concentration is required so I don't make *stupid, idiot moves* when asked by the entity-inside-the-machine which cards I'd like to hold. Too often, I will be deciding whether to hold the low pair or go for the inside straight flush when the lady next to me will say to her slot machine, "Gee, look at that bonus!" And I will [insert the wrong move] because I'm thinking about the woman's interaction with Olive Oyl instead of thinking about my own best move.

Ma'am, I am certain that, at this moment in your life, Olive Oyl is more important than, say, the welfare of your children. But I am engaged in mortal combat at this moment. I'm two points down, there are two seconds left on the clock, and I am taking the ball in my own zone and trying to breeze down the court for a three-point shot to win the game. There are 50 seconds on the clock, and I have the ball, third-and-nine, at the opponent's 40-yard-line. And I'm not handing the ball to Olive Oyl.

Advice Givers
(Slotticus jerkus knowitallus)

These are the busybodies of the slot floor, always nosing around to watch the video poker moves you make or how much is on your credit meter, after which they will make comments designed to demonstrate that they are more knowledgeable concerning the modern electronic slot machine and its proper use than anyone else on the face of the earth.

"Ohh, you gotta go for the flush." "Woah—that was a big hit!" "No, wrong move!"

If you suffer through the presence of an Advice Giver and still manage to score a bit hit, they always give you a warning to heed, sage advice from a master of the slot-playing craft: "Don't give it back to the casino, now."

Uh, thanks.

Cowpokes
(Slotticus jerkus yeehah)

Every so often, no matter where you play slots, you will find yourself surrounded by cowboys. This is especially true if you happen to be in Las Vegas the week of the national rodeo. (Or is it "ro-*day*-oe"?) There will be cowboys all around you, with Western shirts, studded blue jeans, cowboy boots, and zillion-gallon cowboy hats that brush against anyone within, say, 50 yards. Some may be the quiet, Gary Cooper or Jimmy Stewart kind of cowboy, who will sit in stony silence as they face off, at high noon, with the machine.

But there will be many who are like Jerry Jones on steroids, a-pickin' and a-grinnin' and a-slappin' yer back and a-hollerin'.

It will start with you sitting quietly by yourself, engulfed in the relaxing, mesmerizing experience of solitude that slot play can often be. The silence will be broken by a traditional West Texas curse, coming from the direction of the machine next to you: "Sumbitch!" This will be followed a few seconds later with the traditional Central Texas follow-up curse, "*Gott*-damn!" Often, these two terms are deployed together, affected by what is known in English literature as a *metaphorical, reverse-syntax, putting-two-words-together kind of thing*: "*Gott*damn sumbitch!"

What follows is a litany of angst, expressed in successive verses of colloquial hyperbole:

"*Shee*it!"

"What the hayle!"

"What da hayle dey pullin'?"

"*Hott*-damn game is feeixxed!"

"Look at *that*, Junior!"

"Dammm, thang's 'bout to make me crayzee."

"*Gott* . . ."

"*Damn!*"

"Shhheeeitt, how 'bout that, Boss?"

This goes on and on, for a period roughly equivalent to the time it takes for your average cattle drive. Occasionally, though, the drive will hit a stampede when Tex hits a big jackpot, and every player in the casino pauses in abject horror as a siren crashes through the stunned silence:

"EEEEEEEEEEEEEEEEEE-hahh!"

Often, the siren is employed using a slightly altered term, *"Yeee*-hahh." But the result is the same—everyone within 20 feet comes within an inch of a heart attack, and the effect progressively decreases as the blast zone expands and dissipates, from reactions such as chomping through a cocktail glass to, at its outer edge, nothing more serious than mothers whisking their children off the street.

Slot Panther Party
(Slotticus jerkus militus)

There are guys out there on slot floors who are virtual shooting sprees of rage against an institution they refer to only as "the casino." The casino is the enemy and they are preparing to attack. They arrive at the casino prepared for a long siege. When they are playing, this is war. They become jerks only when they start griping. "They never let anyone win!" "Do you believe that? They changed the percentages!"

The common thread holding this subspecies together, though, is mistrust of the casino. To these cats, nothing the casino does is in anything other than its self-interest. Well, okay, they have a point, but these guys raise playing slots or video poker to the level of a military excursion behind enemy lines.

They are convinced the casino exists solely to squeeze every nickel out of every player who walks in the door. Well, okay, they have a point again, but these people take it far too seriously, as if having people win big jackpots here and there is nothing more than a cheap technique to keep everybody else playing in hopes of catching some of that luck, which most of them won't.

Well, you know, that's pretty much how things work, isn't it? How do you join this party?

Chapter 12

Tales from the Road: Vegas

Now that we are all familiar with certain unsavory types of individuals for whom we should be on the lookout, it's time to *hit the road!*

Yes, it is time to move away from the theoretical portion of our little course on the modern slot machine, take everything we have learned thus far, and venture out into the real world of fake backdrops that has been created for us by our "pals" in the casino operations business.

I hope you're ready for our little road trip. I'm sure you have packed your bags, booked your flight, made your hotel reservations, and taken all the sharp objects and C-4 out of the secret compartments in your suitcase.

That's because I told you of our plans last chapter, remember? It was also no doubt included in the publisher's extensive promotional campaign for this book. And then there was the series of TV commercials, starring Alec Baldwin, which must have been created to advertise the book. (That Alec! What a comic genius!)

What you will experience in the next six chapters of our slot opus is a sampling of what is actually out there in the supermarkets of mirth that have been created for us by the "suits" who operate the money factories they call "casinos," and what types of "gaming entertainment" can be had in places around this great nation we call "America," places in which government officials, after looking at their budgets, have made that great philosophical leap: "The hell with raising taxes. Let's just throw up some casinos."

Ah, but no one ever made that leap in the place that is the first stop on our journey, because the casinos in this place were not thrown up by government officials. In this place, the first casinos were thrown up by cowboys, and the next ones were thrown up by guys with names like "Frankie the Fish" and "Johnny No-Nose," and the next by corporate raiders and real estate developers using junk bonds, and the newest ones by corporate bigwigs from huge public companies.

You've probably guessed by now that the first stop on our road trip is the Gaming Capital of the World, Tigre, Argentina. No, wait. That's the Wicker Basket Capital of the World. The gaming capital is Las Vegas, Nevada, a city that always generates the same comment on first glance by travelers from across the globe: "Hey, isn't this the place from *CSI*?"

"Las Vegas" is actually a Spanish term that, of course, means "the Vega," because it is the birthplace of the Chevy Vega. No, wait, wait, that's not right; the term "Las Vegas" means "the Meadows," an obvious reference to the lush, green physical landscape of the area, which evidently did exist at some point back in the Paleolithic period. Unfortunately, ever since humans moved beyond using crude tools to draw cave pictures and courting the opposite sex through a conk on the head with a stone club, the physical landscape of Las Vegas has been more like that of, say, Mercury.

The topographical characteristics of the Las Vegas Valley, in fact, constitute the only reason I have not yet moved my family there. Anyone who lives in Vegas will tell you it is a great place to live. The people telling you that, though, often live either in long-gated, upscale communities or in very old neighborhoods where there has been a lot of time to do things like haul in dirt, plant grass and trees, and generally make things look as if the neighborhoods were *not* located in the middle of a parched desert. In either case, these neighborhoods have been carefully prepared and maintained meticulously so as to resemble the planet Earth, and if constant lawn-watering were ever prohibited they would revert to rattlesnake habitats dotted with stucco houses.

Many people go to Las Vegas in the wintertime, to escape snow and ice and visit a place where daytime outdoor temperatures are in the 50s and 60s during January (which doesn't really matter because all their time will be spent in front of slot machines in environments where indoor temperatures are always in the 70s). But if you really want to get the "full Vegas treatment" visit in July or August. Las Vegas is one of the few cities in America in which newspapers can publish an accurate 30-day weather forecast for any summer month: "Sunny skies. High: 3,000 degrees. Low: 3,000 degrees."

For some real summertime Las Vegas fun, spend a few hours lounging in an air-conditioned room, and then quickly walk outside at about three in the afternoon. For someone from Pittsburgh, this experience induces a blast of nostalgia for the days when steelworkers had to routinely stick their faces into thousand-degree coke ovens. Super-heated air will slam into your body like a sledgehammer, and your stunned vocal chords will manage to squeeze out only a shaky, breathless, two-word phrase:

"Holy . . . shit!"

To enhance this experience, make sure the car you want to drive has been sitting in the sun all day. Initiating a day of travel around town will turn into a fun game known as "Start the Car Before Every Water Molecule in Your Body Evaporates and You Collapse into a Pile of Sticky Goo." What fun! The trip from casino door to car door in itself is like running a race against the Grim Reaper. If you manage to turn the key in the lock without your hand turning into seared meat, you get the "bonus" experience of sitting down on a car seat that is, by now, an upholstered branding iron. Then it's time to play another game: "Try to Drive Without Touching the Ring of Fire That Is the Steering Wheel." Eventually, the air-conditioning kicks in, and the interior temperature of your car eases downward past the 200-degree mark. Then, after a quick stop at the local burn unit, it's off to have some serious casino fun!

The casinos of Las Vegas have transformed a place never meant by God for human habitation into one of the most popular tourist destinations in the world, and, while I may not really want to live there year-round, I absolutely love the place. That's because it is an environment that is uniquely American, which is to say that it is completely artificial. From the neon lights and flashy marquees, to the castles, pirate ships, fountains, and volcanoes, to the go-getter entrepreneurs who hand you seedy porno fliers on the street, it is a fantasy world that has been carefully honed to be like nowhere else on the planet.

It is also a place where anything goes. It is devoid of Victorian hang-ups. No one will suggest that visitors must behave in anything approaching a "moral" fashion. During the 1990s, though, promoters of Las Vegas somehow got the knucklehead idea that the place should be plugged as a "family destination." Thrill rides and theme parks appeared, and the overriding message was "Bring the kids!" Yes, pack little Bobby and Sissy into the minivan and bring them along for some good, clean family fun in the gambling capital of the world! Drunken gamblers started to trip over strollers in casino aisles as yuppie parents carted wide-eyed little scamps past cigar-chomping craps players and rows of men and women lusting for filthy lucre. ("No, Timmy, I don't know what that word means, and, yes, that's what people look like naked. Give me that flier! How many times have I told you not to pick stuff off the ground?")

Thankfully, the city fathers of Las Vegas recently realized that children generally don't spend their allowances at the slots, and that the ability to shed—for at least a few days—all pretense of piety, or sobriety, or "family values," is a big reason people go to Vegas in the first place. The city inaugurated a new promotional campaign—"Las Vegas: What happens here, stays here." It is an attempt to recapture the old "Sin City" image that was carefully crafted to lure tourists in past decades. So now we have commercials showing hung-over Shriners sitting in a Vegas coffee shop wondering where they left one of their buddies:

"Las Vegas. Leave your friend in a ditch somewhere and forget about it. Have another drink."

"Las Vegas. Shoot craps, play the slots, and sleep with a hooker."

"Las Vegas. Just add bourbon."

And, aside from the summertime heat—which, of course, I have exaggerated just a bit (but not much) in an effort to generate a few guffaws—Las Vegas is absolutely, positively, without a doubt, *the best place in the world* to go if you want to play slot machines. Here, with few exceptions, you will find every kind of slot machine known to man. You will also find every kind of casino known to man, except for riverboats and "racinos," and that is *definitely* a good thing. You will find big, luxurious "mega-resort" casinos, stinking little road-house casinos, and everything in between. You will find new slots, old slots, all the video poker you could ever desire—a variety of game choices that exists nowhere else in the world.

And you will find these slot machines *everywhere,* from the moment you step off the plane at McCarron International Airport until you get on another plane to travel back to wherever you came from. You see slots when you stop for gas, when you go to the 7-Eleven, when you stop for groceries, when you go to the dry cleaners, and when you stop to get a burger at a crummy little desert bar. It is Slot-Jockey Heaven.

If you've never been to Vegas, you may find it difficult to com-prehend the fact that slot machines are not restricted to casinos there. One cannot travel two miles in Vegas without encountering a slot. In Nevada, "spare change" is an unknown concept. Casino slot tokens are an acceptable form of contribution when churches pass around the collection plate. The panhandlers accept dollar slot tokens and casino coin coupons. The concept of slot machine play is already familiar to Las Vegans while they are in the womb; most Las Vegas babies come into the world asking for a cocktail and looking for the coin redemption booth.

If you ask me what my favorite place is to play slots in Las Vegas, I will often respond with a stupid look, because I just don't know what to say. (And because I look kind of stupid anyway.) I have many, many favorites in Vegas. I've been going there for almost 20 years now, and I still have much to explore. Every time I go there, they seem to open up a new suburb, with a new suburban casino. As they build Vegas out into the desert, each new suburb crops up like a mining town in the Old West: bank, jail, drug store, hotel, casino. Oh, and strip mall, Starbucks, and In-N-Out Burger.

These are my favorite places to play slots. (The casinos, I mean; not the In-N-Out Burger.) I love the locals hangouts in the sub-urbs. Sam's Town. The Silverton. Sunset Station. Boulder Station. Texas Station. The bus station.

Even if I'm staying in a swank Strip mega-resort, such as the Holiday Inn, I end up going to the locals joints at some point, because these places know that their customers are more interested in the games than in watching a fake volcano or guys dressed up like pirates. When we go to locals joints, ladies and gentlemen, we go to play. We don't feel the need to "be seen," or to dress in the latest from Armani, Gucci, or Old Navy. We come as we are, such as we are, the Great Unwashed Masses of Sparsely Groomed Slot Players, and we *play the freakin' slots.*

Some of these places I like just for their utter lack of pretense or fanciness or big-time promotional hoopla. Take the Silverton. It's down on Blue Diamond Road, south of the airport, in an area that is basically dust, construction vehicles, and new houses, many still being built. It looks like a bunch of suburban American houses that happen to be under construction in Saudi Arabia, and right there by the highway is the Silverton, a little Western lodge–style casino offering your basics—lots of dark wood, multiline video slots, traditional reel-spinners, video poker, a sports bar, and TV monitors around the casino with sports on them. And $2.99 breakfast. What else on Earth do you need?

Right up the street is a little roadhouse bar called the Blue Diamond Saloon, which is even more basic. Pool tables, video poker on the bar, and promotions tallied by the bartender on a chalkboard. Volcanoes? Replicas of Paris and Venice? Hey, this place gives you a six-pack of Bud every time you hit four of a kind in the Bonus Poker games. Now ain't that America! One night, I took a whole case of Bud back to the Strip with me in my rental car, along with the money I'd won from all the quad hands in video poker. Maybe I didn't win ten thousand dollars, but I call that a successful slot session.

I always look for the good little joints, even when I'm staying at Bellagio, Paris, or the Rio. I check into a gorgeous room in Bellagio or the Paris, and walk down the street to Barbary Coast or Bourbon Street to play the slots.

I also love the places that still look like the old sawdust joints. If I can smell the carpet must from the parking lot, I know there are good games in there. Some of the best are still in Downtown Las Vegas, although it's just not the same down in Glitter Gulch since they put up that abomination they call the Fremont Street Experience.

Back in the old days, when you hit Fremont Street you were hitting the quintessential Vegas. Gaudy lights everywhere, the neon cowboy and cowgirl moving their arms against a nighttime sky, those motion lights on the Mint, the corner by Golden Nugget that used to serve as the backdrop for any movie in which a scene was set in Vegas. Then, all the hotels got together and decided they were going to go down in flames if they didn't get more yuppies to come there, and they erected this giant canopy over Fremont Street. The interior surface of the canopy is a computerized video show of fireworks displays, soaring jets, and stuff like that. They shut the entire block off to traffic, so now you have these classic sawdust joints with open fronts like the Fremont and Binion's Horseshoe, opening onto what resembles a mall somewhere in Jersey. And the neon cowboy looks as if he's pointing to the spot on his back that hurts because he's all scrunched into the corner of a ceiling.

The games inside are still good, though. You find good nickel and quarter video slots, decent video poker, and smoky, dark rooms that still look like a casino ought to look. That's if you can find a place to park. You see, shutting off four blocks to traffic had a fun side effect: it is now easier to find a parking space in New York City than in Downtown Las Vegas. You can still park in, say, the Four Queens parking garage, which has ramps and parking spaces that seem to have been designed for go-carts. But outside of the hotel parking garages, well, let's just say you should go at five in the morning, park your car, and take a cab back later.

Still, I do have my favorites Downtown, as I do in every other subdivision of Las Vegas. So, to communicate some of my "Vegas Tales," I will now take you on a theoretical road trip around the gaming capital, cramming my thousands of Vegas experiences into a composite romp through the best darned slot town in the world.

It all starts at McCarron Airport. You'll hear the *ding-ding* of the slots as you walk up the Jetway from your plane, then you'll see large airport waiting areas stuffed with a variety of slot games. Here's what you should do: *keep walking*. The payback percentage policy at the airport was developed to take advantage of the fact that people often lose a lot of money in Vegas, and may want to make one last, desperate attempt to recoup losses before they get on their planes. Many of the games out there take advantage of the fact that slots are legally allowed to pay back as little as 75 percent in Nevada. They are generally set on "suck." The best games you will find are dollar Bonus Poker games, with the 7/5 pay table that only "kind of sucks," and those are concentrated in the "smoker's pen," that hermetically sealed jail cell they throw you into if you dare to think you may want to ignite a tobacco product in the airport.

I'll tell you more about airport slots on our return journey, but for now just pass them right by, and get to your cab or rental car. There is no reason in the world for you to stop on the way into town, with all your casino slot money, and play these stinkers. Unless you want to go through all your money immediately and end up watching Regis in your hotel room all week. (And yes, I have done that. But not from playing at the airport.)

For our first foray into the world of Vegas slot play beyond the airport, we'll go to a few of my favorite locals joints. What you should do is check out the suburbs surrounding the Strip, one at a time. In the southeast is Boulder Highway, and for me that means Sam's Town. The first time I went to Sam's was in 1984, when it was called "Sam's Town Saloon, Casino, Dance Hall, and Western Emporium with Cowboys, Cowboy Hats, Straight Whiskey, Six-Shooters, and Cowpokes A-Moseyin' Around." Well, it was something to that effect, anyway. It was a veritable hoe-down of a casino, with rustic wood beams all over the place and "both kinds of music—country *and* Western." All right, maybe the music did not appeal to my own tastes, which lean toward Mozart, Bach, and Marilyn Manson, but I always had a blast at the place.

Sam's Town has changed a lot since those days. In the '90s, they added what is now called the Mystic Falls Indoor Park, a wonderful fake nature preserve facing the registration desk. It is an indoor park under a huge glass atrium, with hotel rooms surrounding it that have windows overlooking the atrium so you can gaze out on the fake park. At one side is a huge fake rock formation, and a fake cave that houses a fake wolf. (Or maybe it's a fake coyote; I'm not sure.) The animal stars in a big laser and light show that periodically delights patrons, and ends with the fake critter howling at a fake moon. If you are ever staying at Sam's in one of the interior rooms and decide to go to bed early (I know that's a stretch), you will be blasted out of your bed with a near–heart attack when the show starts with music blaring at a volume level that simulates a jet engine, or a Who concert.

There are shops all around the ground level of the park, including the buffet, which lamentably replaced what had been the best sports bar in town. But at least now you can sit in the buffet eating scrambled eggs while watching a fake woodpecker peck at fake wood.

One thing that has not changed at Sam's Town is that there are great slots (and so-so video poker games), with some of the best payback percentages in the city. Another thing that has not changed is that *everyone is friendly.* Cowpoke friendly. Down-home friendly. On-the-verge-of-nauseating friendly.

You notice the friendliness if you park yourself at a bar and play bar-top slots or video poker. I did this once for a period that lasted, like, a week, during which I talked to every bartender in the place for hours at a time. They're all on my Christmas list now, because I won a thousand dollars at the bar on two different occasions.

From Sam's Town, it is a short drive to the suburb of Henderson, and another of my favorite locals joints, Sunset Station. You may go to Vegas for luxurious high-roller suites and Wayne Newton concerts, but you've still got to love a casino that includes a movie theater and a Fatburger. (I am proud to say that Sunset Station was the scene of my very first Fatburger experience, during which I marveled at my own ability to entirely consume a hamburger the size of a mature ape.)

Sunset Station is one of the best places in the city to find new games, because slot manufacturers often use it as a site for "beta tests." (As opposed to "VHS tests"—you'll get that joke if you're old like me.) These are field tests performed on new games as the final step in the approval process. The regulators put games out for these field trials to ensure that they perform as the manufacturers say they do, and to gauge any potential problems, such as sharp edges that cut into player flesh, or those pesky exploding top boxes, which send shards of broken glass outward in all directions.

No, seriously, field trials are usually a formality at the end of the approval process to ensure that everything works correctly, and legally, in a new slot game. So at Sunset Station you can play many games that can be found nowhere else.

It was this way with the Three Stooges, a video slot produced by IGT and Shuffle Master Gaming. I had written of the plans for this game, but had not seen it in a casino until one day when I was wandering around Sunset Station, trying to walk off some blubber after scarfing down a Fatburger. I was walking along listening to the *ding-ding* of traditional games when I heard the unmistakable, soothing voice of Moe Howard calling someone a "knucklehead," or a "chowderhead," or some other kind of head. What I encountered next were hilarious head-bonks, nose-twists, eye-gouges, face-slaps, ear-tweaks, and calls of "woo-woo-woo." Then, after security guards removed the disturbed player who was doing all of this, I checked out the Three Stooges slot. (Nyuk-nyuk!)

The slot floor at Sunset Station is huge, and the variety of video slots is unmatched. There is also some very good video poker to be had. Oh, and there's a fake sky too, so it looks like you're playing outdoors at sunset. (Get it?)

Sunset Station was also the home of the very first Beat the House seminar, an event that treated players to two days of talks by all of my expert-gaming-writer pals. I gave a talk there, too, in which I basically outlined chapter 6 of this book, the one about slot myths. I'm afraid I wasn't nearly as funny as the chapter, though. I have a deep-seated fear of public speaking, particularly when it's just me, by myself, talking to a roomful of strangers. Public speaking always makes me feel like I'm about to address the UN and I suddenly realize that I'm wearing a clown suit. If you attended that talk, I'm sorry I wasn't all that funny. Truth is, I was petrified. My wife had told me that I'd be fine if I just pictured you all sitting there in your underwear, but that turned out to be even scarier than speaking.

To make matters worse, I followed Frank Scoblete, the gaming expert who edited and wrote the foreword to this book, and a man for whom public speaking is second nature. Scoblete had the crowd in the palm of his hand, and then on I walked, a quivering blob of nerves. I felt like Ralph Kramden when he went on TV and could only say, "Hummina-hummina-hummina."

But, getting back to our road trip, let's leave Sunset Station and get on one of the Vegas highways (an experience that is either like a high-speed movie car chase or a crowded mall parking lot, depending on the time of day) to go to the very best locals joints in town, up in the northwest suburbs. Here, you will find more Station casinos— Santa Fe Station, Texas Station, and Fiesta Rancho (which used to be Fiesta Station, after it was just Fiesta). Also here, you will find the highest payback percentages on slots anywhere in the country, along with high-payback video poker, friendly people, and strip malls and gas stations and houses and stuff like that.

Inside these casinos, you will find various "themes," such as tacos and sombreros at Fiesta, a hacienda motif at Santa Fe, and rootin'-tootin', highfalutin cowboy stuff at Texas. But none of that matters, because there are tons of great slots with good variety and high paybacks at all three, and they're all hooked up to one of the best slot clubs in town, the Boarding Pass program.

As we get closer to the Strip, we have to stop at some great locals places just west of the Big Road. On West Tropicana, don't miss the Orleans. It has a massive floor, chock full of great slot games and a sea of video poker machines. (Although the pay tables on video poker are not nearly as good as they were a few years ago, thanks to a baffling policy of parent Coast Casinos apparently designed to drive away good business.) I love the Orleans because it's minutes from the airport, so it always offers a great "last-chance" stop at the end of a trip. I once had an hour to kill before going to the airport, at the end of a trip on which I was a couple of hundred down. I threw a $20 bill into a quarter Bonus Poker machine and hit the royal—a cool grand in my pocket with no time to give it back to the casino. *That's* what I'm talkin' about!

Then, on West Flamingo, we've got to stop at the Palms. This is sort of a hybrid between a locals joint and a tourist spot. There are great slots and video poker with locals-style paybacks, along with trendy tourist attractions like the Ghost Bar, where the Beautiful People can get blitzed and go out on the terrace for a kick-ass view of the Strip at night, along with vertigo from standing on this one square of glass through which you can see the pavement a zillion feet below. Try that after three martinis for a real thrill. (It may be a good idea to have a barf bag at the ready.)

Then there's the Rio, also on West Flamingo, which is really a Strip mega-resort that happens to be off the Strip. You should check it out for the standard rooms alone, which are all suites, and for a great collection of the newest multiline video slots.

Before we get to our final destination, the Strip, we have to stop a couple of blocks from that famous street at my very favorite casino in Las Vegas, the Hard Rock on Paradise Road. It's not that this place necessarily has the best slot games in town, although it does have some good video poker games. It is simply my favorite place to play because it is *major cool*. At least to a writer like me who also happens to nurture a lifetime obsession with rock and roll music. There are guitars displayed everywhere—not just guitars, but the guitars of my heroes, signed by my heroes. Hendrix. The Stones. The Who. Clapton. Slim Whitman.

Even their clothes are on display—everything from Elvis's jumpsuits to stage costumes of the Guy Formerly Known as the Artist Formerly Known as Prince, Who Is Now Known as Prince Again the Last I Heard.

You can play slots at the Hard Rock to a soundtrack of the very best rock music ever recorded, and not just the big Top 40 hits either. Win or lose, *I be jammin'* when I play in this place.

Oh, and let's not forget the babes.

Not that I would ever notice, mind you, since I am a happily married man and, as such, am automatically and permanently blinded to any potentially appealing physical characteristics of any woman of the female persuasion, other than my lovely bride. But from what I have . . . umm . . . "heard," at around 7 P.M. on any given evening, the Hard Rock becomes absolutely stuffed with gorgeous, scantily clad, 25-year-old women who all have bodies which would, in the words of legendary bluesman Willie Dixon, "make a preacherman lay his Bible down." On weekends, they pour into the Hard Rock like hot asphalt being poured onto a stretch of Mississippi highway in July—young beauties blazing with scorching heat and just itching to party the night away, drinking and twisting their glistening bodies seductively to erotic, pounding rock and roll rhythms.

Well, that's what I've heard, anyway.

We will now drive out of the Hard Rock. After a couple of minutes employing a frenzied, manic driving technique, we reach the epicenter of the gaming capital—Las Vegas Boulevard. The Strip. The legendary stomping grounds of Frank, Dean, and Sammy. The street where they had the Summit at the Sands (which isn't there anymore). The site of the five casinos (two of which aren't there anymore) on which the Rat Packers pulled off the heist in the original *Oceans Eleven*. The site of Bugsy Siegel's Flamingo (or, in *The Godfather*, Moe Greene's Tropigala). The site of the Stardust of Lefty Rosenthal and Tony the Ant Spilotro (you know . . . the Tangiers of Ace Rothstein and Nicky Santoro in *Casino*).

The Strip—the movie-set landscape of giant fantasy megaresorts that distinguish today's Las Vegas from any other city on Earth.

From a skilled gambler's point of view, the Strip doesn't offer the slot player the best payback percentages in town, but you will still find incredible variety in game selection—the best anywhere, in fact. That's because the casinos know that *everybody* goes there. Even if you prefer locals casinos, one should not—cannot—visit Vegas without hitting the Strip. To do Vegas right, at some point you'll have to go see Danny Gans at the Mirage, Wayne Newton at the Stardust, David Copperfield at the MGM, Buddy Guy or B.B. King at the House of Blues, the fountains at Bellagio, cocktail waitresses dressed like Roman slaves at Caesars Palace, and Gotham street scenes inside New York–New York. You can't go to Vegas and avoid the Strip. It's the law. So put on your best Hawaiian shirt, Bermuda shorts, straw hat, and sunglasses, grab your camera, and let's do the tourist thing!

Before we start, a general opinion of slot play on the Strip: You'll find the newest games and great selection at all the mega-resorts, but, if it's the highest payback percentages you seek, just breeze through for the tourist attractions and head back to the locals casinos to play. To put things in perspective, overall slot payback percentage for the entire group of Strip properties is generally around 92 percent, whereas the locals casinos in North Las Vegas, on the Boulder Strip, and on the outskirts of the county generally offer between 95 and 96 percent payback overall. It may not seem like a significant difference—and you may not notice it in the short term, particularly if you hit a big jackpot—but long-term, day-to-day, serious slot jockeys should stick with the places where the locals play.

But you still have to visit the Strip. Like I said before, it's the law.

To start your Strip tour properly, drive all the way down Paradise, exit to Sunset Road, and turn right on Las Vegas Boulevard to approach the casinos from the south. That will take you past the famous "Welcome to *Fabulous* Las Vegas" sign, which was saved from extinction just a few years ago by local preservationists. So you can still get the classic tourist photo of you standing next to the sign in your shorts and funny hat, waving and smiling at the camera like a doofus.

After you get the picture, drive for a few seconds and take a left into the southernmost mega-resort on the Strip, Mandalay Bay. Physically, it is a stunning place, inside and out. The coolest thing to do there outside of the casino floor is to find someone you know who is rich and/or important, and is therefore a member of the Foundation Room private club in the House of Blues. If you can tag along with them to the Foundation Room like some low-rent syco-phant who attaches himself to more affluent people (Hey, just like me!), you can drink yourself into stupor in a club that includes a terrace offering the quintessential view of the Strip at night. It is a view you've probably seen a million times on TV shows like *CSI*, only this time you're there seeing it for yourself. Just remember to go out on the terrace first, and drink later. After a few of those Foundation Room martinis, you may think nothing of climbing over the terrace railing and doing a Spider-Man impersonation on the side of the hotel.

But even if you don't know anyone rich or important there are plenty of places to drink yourself stupid at Mandalay Bay. Red Square comes to mind immediately. It's all done up like Soviet Russia, complete with a concrete façade and a statue of Lenin in front, the head of which was broken off and stolen shortly after the restaurant opened (still an unsolved case). The story is that Mandalay officials thought the statue looked even cooler decapitated, so they just left it in place.

You can eat at Red Square, but drinking there is much more fun. You can arrange to get a coat and go into a deep-freeze cooler to drink various Russian vodkas, or choose from a menu of a zillion flavored martinis, each tasting like fruit punch and each packing a wallop strong enough to put Boris Yeltsin on his backside.

There's also: the "3950" club, which beams sporting events to video screens on the walls of single-person restrooms (Now, how cool is *that*?); the ultra-hip "rumjungle" club; and China Grill, where you can get an exotic cocktail that comes in a glass the size of a large fishbowl, and subsequently stagger back to your room like Otis the Town Drunk.

But enough about the opportunities to imbibe at Mandalay—this is a slot book. And for slot variety, no place is better. Like Sunset Station, Mandalay Bay is a popular beta-test site for new games, so there are lots of opportunities to play exclusive new slots. In addition, at Mandalay you will always find one of the best overall selections of slots in the nation. While video poker players will find pay table selection lousy—it is a tourist place, after all—the straight slot player will never run out of things to discover.

Oh, and before you leave check out the only "beach" in the Mojave Desert—a wave pool surrounded by a sand "shoreline." *Viva Las Vegas* . . .

Next door to Mandalay is its sister property, the Luxor, with its pyramid-shaped hotel, dressed in an exterior light show that sends dramatic laser beams into the nighttime sky. Inside, it is all done up like ancient Egypt, as if Ramses had commissioned slaves to build the "Pharaoh's Casino, Hotel, and Resort" inside his palace. Long gone is the confusing New York City mockup that was featured inside the casino when the place first opened. (Too many people said, "Huh?") But in addition to the Egypt theme they do have a cool thrill ride there—a "virtual reality" trip through a mineshaft in a railroad car, which can sometimes cause the "non-virtual reality" effect of losing one's lunch.

As far as the slots go, there is a pretty good selection of games, although it's not nearly as good as at Mandalay.

The next stop on the Strip is a cluster of resorts surrounding the intersection of Las Vegas Boulevard and Tropicana Avenue, often called the "New Four Corners." The old Four Corners was the intersection of Fremont Street and Casino Center Boulevard in Downtown Las Vegas, which offered the famous Glitter Gulch neon-jungle nighttime tableau of the Golden Nugget, Four Queens, Fremont, and Binion's Horseshoe—before it was all ruined by the Fremont Street Experience. Now, the southernmost major intersection of the Strip has claimed the Four Corners title, because it is surrounded by the Tropicana, MGM Grand, New York–New York, and Excalibur. Slot play at all of these places is basically typical Strip—fantastic game selection, yard upon yard of incredible variety, and percentages and video poker pay tables that elicit a huge yawn.

But the settings in which all these slots are placed is what make these resorts something special. Well, all except the Tropicana. That resort was last refurbished with a new design in 1986, when it went from its old "Tiffany of the Strip" image to the tropical "Island of Las Vegas" theme, with live cockatoos and parrots and other exotic birds perched around all the public walkways. The theme—and the average Trop hotel room, for that matter—has become old, tired, and threadbare, and the exotic birds must be on Social Security by now. ("*Squawk* . . . Cough! Cough!")

I do still like playing at the Trop, though, partly because its slot club has some of the coolest promotions around—many, like the tic-tac-toe-playing chickens, exported from the Atlantic City Tropicana—and partly because of sentimental reasons: my wife and I had our honeymoon there in the 1980s. (My marriage has held up *much* better than the Trop, by the way.)

From the Trop, we can go to the other three "corners" by traversing elevated walkways, installed some years back to address the rising danger to pedestrians of getting squashed like bugs trying to cross the Strip. The MGM Grand is simply incredible, not only for its Hollywood fantasy theme, but for its sheer size. The first time I went into the place, I actually got lost inside. I kept walking and walking, and only found more and more casino. I finally did emerge several weeks later, with a long beard, tattered clothing, and my hands gnarled from continuous slot play. By that point, there were milk cartons around town bearing my picture.

Across the Strip from MGM is New York–New York, a must-see replica of New York City, its exterior adorned with scaled-down versions of the Chrysler Building, the Statue of Liberty and other Gotham landmarks, its interior a collection of replica street scenes from the Big Apple. It is definitely a fun place to walk around, and another prime spot for all of the newest slot games in the industry. At the very top of the outer structure is a Coney Island–style roller coaster that snakes around the exterior at what seems like a mile in the air. It is no doubt the setting of many horrific scenes involving lunches lost in the wind. Across Tropicana from that property is Excalibur, a replica of a medieval castle complete with jousting shows. Beside the theme itself, there is not a lot to say about the casino, other than the facts that it has good Strip-style selection and that, on my last visit at least, it was in dire need of a facelift.

Traveling northward on the Strip, you will find a mix of old and new leading you into the center of town. First on the left is Monte Carlo, a joint venture of MGM Mirage and Mandalay Resorts that is like your typical Steve Wynn property—wonderful, luxurious rooms, so-so slots and video poker (good game selection, though), and great restaurants. Next to that is the Boardwalk, an older casino with an exterior recalling East Coast wooden seaside walkways and their amusement offerings, while offering more of a locals-casino feel on the inside (except for the game selection, which is pretty pathetic). For all you road-weary travelers, there is a Holiday Inn hotel attached. On the other side of the street is the Aladdin, which was recently imploded and completely rebuilt and redesigned into one of the most confusing configurations of a multileveled casino you'll ever find. (We're all waiting for the next implosion.)

North of that are the casinos leading to the heart of the Strip mega-resort district—Bellagio on one side and sister properties Paris Las Vegas and Bally's Las Vegas on the other, followed by an incredible lineup of must-see mega-resorts sprinkled with little locals-style casinos and grand old properties. It's an amazing string of stuff—on the west side, Caesars Palace, Mirage, Treasure Island. On the east side, Barbary Coast, the Flamingo, Imperial Palace, Harrah's, Casino Royale, and, on the hallowed ground of the old Sands, the Venetian.

Most of these are the most famous modern-day tourist spots in Vegas, and the serious slot player should visit them not just to play slots, but also for the experience. It's Vegas law that, at some point, you must see the fake volcano outside of the Mirage, or the epic sea battle at Treasure Island (which is now known by the trendier nickname "TI"). You've got to go gawk at the scaled-down Eiffel Tower and victory arch at Paris, although, trust me, all the French stuff inside will soon become annoying—the way they say *Bonjour!* when you call to the front desk for a new hair dryer, the security guards in the silly French pillbox hats, and *definitely* the roaming mimes, who you just want to slap.

You've got to go to Caesars Palace to experience what are, for my money, still the best standard hotel rooms on the Strip, and to go on a shopping jag in the amazing Forum Shops. You've got to see the Flamingo to look at the plaque commemorating murderous mobster and Vegas pioneer Bugsy Siegel, and the location of what used to be Bugsy's suite—foolishly torn down some years back to make room for the new pool area. (After you see that, leave. There's nothing much to speak of game-wise, and they have jerks selling time-shares by the hotel elevators.)

You should stop in the Imperial Palace to see the classic auto collection—a cool way to entertain oneself without diminishing the bankroll. I've met some strange characters over the years at the IP, though. One night, my wife and I were at the bar talking to another couple, having a great time, when out of the blue the other couple invited us up to their room to "party." We respectfully declined the offer, and then got to thinking: who invites complete strangers to their hotel rooms in the middle of the night? We imagined whips, chains, and meat cleavers, after which our bodies would most likely have been chopped into pieces and put into blenders to create a side dish for their room-service meal. Anyhoo . . .

Before you leave town, you *must* walk through the Venetian, not for the façades replicating Venice or the gondoliers pushing their boats around the fake waterway, but for the interior architecture. It is an amazing, museum-quality, intricate crafting of an interior design. Simply beautiful. If you stay in the hotel, you will find gorgeous split-level suites as the standard rooms. Most of us, though, have to wait until we hit a jackpot at another property to stay at the Venetian, or take out a loan to pay the room rates.

My personal favorite spot to play slots in the mega-resort district is Barbary Coast, because it is an old-style, sawdust-joint locals casino plopped in the middle of the posh hotel district. Limits are low, slot payback percentages are high. As I said before, I usually escape to either there or Bourbon Street, just off the Strip, for more sane, locals-style slot play when I'm staying at Bally's or the Bellagio.

As for the Bellagio, it is probably, overall, my favorite place to stay on the Strip. Aside from perhaps Caesars Palace and the Venetian, you won't find a more luxurious standard room anywhere in town, and the property is simply amazing. It is also, I must admit, my "lucky" slot spot on the Strip. I once came out a thousand bucks ahead two nights in a row there. I know, I know. It means nothing with respect to future play. But, hey, I'm allowed to be superstitious once in a while just like you. So lighten up.

Traveling farther up the Strip, you will find all of the classic older casino hotels—New Frontier, Stardust, Westward Ho, and Circus Circus on the west side; Riviera and Sahara on the east. Also on the east side is the site of the old Desert Inn, which was torn down to make room for Steve Wynn's latest project, Wynn Las Vegas. It all ends up with the Stratosphere on the north end of the Strip—a fun place that was more fun when it was the old Bob Stupak's Vegas World, which boasted the best promotions in town (and the most fabulously gaudy interior design as well).

For my money, play on the north end is usually concentrated at the Sahara, which was recently renovated with a brand-new design, and the Stardust, probably the most well-preserved of the legendary Vegas casinos.

Oh, and a block away from the Strip on the north end is the Las Vegas Hilton. Don't bother.

If you've made it this far, dear reader, you are standing with me inside the Stratosphere, wondering whether to venture farther north. Again, don't bother, unless you want to get married Vegas-style. Between the Stratosphere and the Downtown casino center are all the drive-in wedding chapels, and lots of seedy neighborhoods surrounding them. And, although there are great casinos like Binion's and Four Queens and Fremont Downtown, I'd just rather not deal with the "Experience." So it's time to go up to the restaurant at the top of the Stratosphere, pay $50 for a meal as the restaurant rotates to give you a last, panoramic view of all of Las Vegas, rid yourself of that $50 meal with a "gravity trip" up and down the "Space Needle," and then head back to McCarron Airport.

I did win once at the airport, an experience I related in a *Strictly Slots* column. I played one of the 7/5 Bonus Poker games I mentioned before, and I hit four Aces for four hundred dollars. As dollar tokens clanged into the hopper, it was almost time for my flight, and, naturally, the hopper emptied. After waiting for an attendant for an excruciatingly long time and waiting at the redemption booth for another excruciatingly long time as the zombie cashier moved in slow motion, I managed to jump onto the plane just before it took off.

But I had won at the airport, a first in the history of the casino industry. And one great way to speed off to the next stop on our road trip, Atlantic City, New Jersey, with its hip new slogan, "Always Turned On."

But first, one more little Vegas tale:

In the posh Strip mega-resorts, one thing you find is that, if you are of the male persuasion, sometimes as you play slots you will be approached by women who are, as they say, "working." They assume that if you're staying there you have money. I once had a beautiful woman initiate a conversation that made me consider the possibility that a balding, middle-aged man is really what the hot babes are looking for these days. Then, after complimenting me on my shirt or my mustache or something, she casually asked me if I was a cop. That's when my ego came crashing back to harsh reality, and to a choice between asking for a price menu or politely excusing myself. I chose the latter.

Hey, at least for a brief, shining moment, I got to thinking I was still a babe magnet.

Chapter 13

Tales from the Road:
Atlantic City

It is now time to visit the Second City of Casino Gambling in America: Atlantic City, New Jersey. It was May of 1978 when polyester-clad patrons lined up around the block to enter the first Atlantic City casino, Resorts International, and experience its sea of Bally slots and table games. The first legal American casino east of Nevada officially opened when singer Steve Lawrence tossed the bones onto a Resorts International craps table (looking like Sky Masterson from *Guys and Dolls*) as Eydie waited patiently at a slot machine with all the other women.

Before that fateful day, Atlantic City was on a prolonged deathwatch. The grand old hotels—which had been the gems of the East back in Atlantic City's swing-era heyday, when it was known as the "Queen of Resorts"—had spent most of the 1970s catering to a few stumblebums, while the famed Boardwalk, once the most vibrant Eastern entertainment center outside of New York City, played host to seedy souvenir shops and T-shirt stands. Away from the Boardwalk was a town full of boarded-up houses and failed businesses. Casino gaming was seen as a savior for the city.

It did take a while for the saving to take hold. For the first few years, as spanking new casinos cropped up along the Boardwalk, the dilapidated houses and boarded-up businesses nearby provided photo-ops for countless "rich-man-poor-man," "slums-by-the-gaming-palaces" articles. But New Jersey gaming law had a provision that devoted a portion of casino profits to civic improvements; when it took hold, Atlantic City went through a renaissance of construction outside the casinos—a building boom that created brand-new dilapidated houses and boarded-up businesses.

No, I'm kidding. Today's Atlantic City is a great place to visit, and even a nice place to live. It has a new convention center, tidy new housing all over the place, and a Boardwalk that is undergoing constant improvement. Some 30 million people a year visit Atlantic City. Then they go home. You see, unlike Vegas, Atlantic City is still largely a regional market, drawing drive-in patrons from all of the densely populated Northeast Corridor states. (The dense population is, however, gradually being replaced by a smarter population.)

In Atlantic City, a wealth of business is generated by day-trippers and one-night visitors, as opposed to weeklong vacationers. This is all changing, though. For years, the casinos have been trying to redefine the market as a "destination resort," a place where people come for a week instead of a day. This process began to move into high gear in the summer of 2003 when Borgata, a Vegas-style mega-resort, opened in the marina district—located, in an interesting symbolic twist, on the site of the former city dump.

But enough of the civic history lesson. Like I said before, this is a slot book. So let's see what all this Atlantic City casino hoopla is about by driving our cars down the Atlantic City Expressway (average speed: 120) toward the slot palaces of Atlantic City.

First, a few general observations on the Atlantic City market:

Overall, the slots are stingier than in Nevada, by around 3 percentage points. By comparison, in 2002 casinos with the loosest slots in Nevada returned an overall 95.46 percent of all the money wagered, while the most generous Atlantic City slot house, Resorts, returned 92.26 percent overall. This is due to one word: competition. Nevada has hundreds of casinos, which means that each one is looking for that edge to draw patrons across the street, and loose slots are a big draw. In Atlantic City, there are 12 casinos (if you count Bally's, which is really three casinos, as one, and Trump Plaza, which is two casinos, as another one). There simply is not the same kind of competitive pressure here as in Nevada.

The 3 percent difference in payback is certainly significant over the long run, even though Atlantic City slot clubs have always made up the difference by offering more cash back and comps than Nevada casinos. This has been changing lately. Cash back and comps are shrinking as the marketing emphasis shifts from loose slots to resort amenities, so the gap between the two markets again is widening.

And don't forget that 92.26 percent is the cream of the market. In most cases—particularly with the nickel multiline video slots—you're playing games that return around 90 percent. Put another way, you're giving up a whopping 10 percent house edge when you play nickel slots in Atlantic City.

(Atlantic City panhandlers, by the way, return around 0.0 percent.)

In the market's defense, though, with few exceptions the percentages in Atlantic City are within a point or two of the returns you'll find anywhere in the nation except for Nevada. That's because, outside of Nevada (where slots are everywhere), what you have around the country are generally small, regional markets, rarely with more than a dozen or so casino choices.

But, hey, these are slots, right? You already know going in that you're not going to get a small house edge like you get in blackjack or baccarat, or a player-advantage game like you can get in the best video poker. You're playing slots because you love them. In most areas of the country, the high house edge is the nature of the beast. You can placate yourself with the knowledge that, if you need an alternative to the high house edge, the Nevada locals casinos are always there for you.

Personally, I love Atlantic City, partly because I have been intimately involved with the place for years. My professional life is based there, and though I do love Vegas it's always nice to get back to familiar casinos in a part of the country that is fit for human habitation in the summertime, where these things they call "trees" grow naturally, and where you can go to a beach that was not created by a casino vendor.

I even love the aspects of Atlantic City that have been criticized from time to time. The Boardwalk has all these kitschy souvenir shops where you can buy stuff like little mechanical weasels that flip and flop around, or T-shirts bearing philosophical slogans such as "Bite Me," or any variety of useless, fun junk. In the summertime, the carnies come out with midway games on the boards and amusement rides on the piers. You can ride between casinos in the legendary rolling chairs, which in bygone days were pushed by men wearing tuxedos but are now often operated by guys who look sort of like terrorists. (But they're friendly terrorists, and their only terror is usually the price they charge.)

Oh, and let's not forget the "colorful" characters you often encounter on the Boardwalk. Musicians jamming for coins. Ragged men having intense conversations with themselves as they walk. (Even their imaginary friends have imaginary friends.) I once saw a guy standing by Trump Plaza in the morning painting himself from head to toe with silver paint. I went back the same way in the afternoon and he was doing a perfect impersonation of a statue. I mean, he *nailed* it. I gave him five bucks.

Gypsy fortunetellers are another fun species. They'll offer to read one palm for a buck, or two for five dollars. I always thought they should give a volume discount for two palms—you know, two for $1.50—but the lady at the "House of Knowledge" told me they can get much more information about you if they read two palms. (I told her to read my feet too, and tell me my entire future life story.) When they read your palms or, for the really deluxe $10 story of your life, tarot cards, you will always be told that you're going to get a new job, that your financial situation is going to get better, and that you will achieve happiness in your love life. (Just once, I'd like them to tell somebody they're going to get hit by a bus next Tuesday.) There is only one prediction they make, though, that is guaranteed to be accurate: "You will now give me five dollars."

As you walk down the Boardwalk (we'll get to the Marina district later), you encounter signature items that can only be found on the Jersey shore, which Easterners claim as vital links to their cultural heritage. Fat-filled, please-give-me-a-heart-attack foods like cheese steaks, gargantuan cuts of pizza, corn dogs, and chili dogs fill the summer air with the smell of Jersey. Hey, just *try* to get a decent cheese steak or corn dog in Vegas. Or for that matter, saltwater taffy.

But, getting back to the slots (oh, yeah—it's a slot book), one aspect of Atlantic City slot play that is on the move is the "coin-free" revolution. Park Place Entertainment properties started this trend in 2001 by introducing ticket printers on a few banks of games at Bally's Wild Wild West casino annex. Now, almost half the slots at Bally's have ticket printers, and the company, which changed its name to Caesars Entertainment at the beginning of 2004, is introducing them gradually at all its other Atlantic City properties. (They own three, which are really five if you count the annex properties. Plus, I think they own the Atlantic Ocean.) The Borgata opened with a totally coin-free slot floor, and aside from the eerie quiet of the place people seem to be enjoying it.

Ticket-printing slots accept bills but pay out by printing a secure ticket that can be redeemed at the cage or used in another slot. The casinos love them, because they don't have any coin-handling costs. As for us players, some of us love them, others are gradually warming to them, and some hate them.

Those of us who love coin-free play feel this way because we have had our fill (no pun intended) of lousy coin service in Atlantic City. There are Atlantic City casinos in which the task of transporting a sack of quarters across the floor appears to be more difficult than resolving the Israeli-Palestinian conflict.

You will be cheerfully spinning your reels when you decide it's time to quit. You hit the cash-out button, and your coins fall steadily into the tray until—and I think this is a rule—it stops with less than $10 left on the meter, triggering that that all-too-familiar message, "Hopper Empty. Call Attendant." You say, "Attendant! Attendant!" and get no answer. That's because the message "Call Attendant" is little more than a cruel joke, since there are maybe two attendants employed to cover a slot floor containing two thousand machines. Eventually, an attendant will show up, but not with a sack of quarters. The attendant is there to open the door of the slot and see if you *really* need more quarters, to make sure you're not just trying to pull some practical joke on the casino.

They see there are maybe 10 quarters in the hopper, and swirl them around with a pen to make more quarters fall out. They close the door, reset the machine, and two quarters drop. They open the door again, and proceed to fill out paperwork that is similar in volume to the United States Tax Code. Then they disappear again, because they have to go to the cage and wait for a security guard to accompany them and the sack of quarters back to your machine. Mind you, this whole time, the sacred quarters are maybe 12 feet from where you are sitting, and through computers they knew ahead of time that your particular machine needed a hopper fill, and what denomination of coins was needed. But "these are the procedures we have to follow," they will tell you.

Oh, and after your machine gets its hopper filled you're not done. Because now, after your cash-out is complete, you have to scoop the coins into buckets and carry the buckets, each of which approximates the weight of a block of pig iron, to the Seventh Level of Hell that is coin redemption, where you get to stand in line as each person is served by cashiers whose limbs move at the same speed as a tree growing to maturity.

So I, for one, was happy to see coin-free play initiated in Atlantic City. You may disagree with me, and you do have valid points. Handling coins after a big jackpot is part of the "slot experience." You like to immerse your filthy paws into that pile of moolah after you win. You love the *clang-clang* of those quarters or dollar tokens hitting the metal hopper tray, and, let's face it, that lame *ching-ching* sound that the coin-free slots make as the tickets print out just doesn't cut it.

But, for the Atlantic City market, the cure is *definitely* better than the disease. And, after the Borgata has been around for a while, other casinos in town are sure to go coin-free, so your best course of action is to just get over it and play the slots.

Before getting into my view of the best and worst places to play in Atlantic City, I have a couple more general observations. First, watch out for the elderly. Atlantic City's motto is "Where Life Begins at 90." Retirees drive there and mosey up Pacific Avenue in their cars, maintaining average speeds of 15 miles per hour. They take their Social Security checks and flock there on buses. If you go into an Atlantic City casino late in the morning, it looks like a reunion of Gettysburg veterans. If you happen to be near the bus lobby in Showboat at about 11 A.M. when the buses open their doors, it's like a jailbreak at the rest home. You will suddenly be immersed in a geriatric sea, attempting to navigate your way through a gray herd of ostensibly confused senior citizens, each taking a few minutes to contemplate his or her next step.

Oh, I'm kidding. I love the retirees, because they are always, always happy. No mortgage, kids long gone, no boss, no work to do . . . nothing to do but hang in a casino and play the slots. Hey, I'd be happy too. And I plan to be right there with them in around 30 years, with my fanny pack, my Depends, my support stockings, and my Social Security check, playing the slots and pitying the poor schmucks who have to drag themselves to an office every day.

Another general observation is that the slot selection is usually great in any given Atlantic City casino. As with Las Vegas, you will always find a good selection of the newest slot games. It was not always this way. Only a few years ago, Atlantic City was among the last places in the country to get new slot games, but nowadays, thanks to changes in the regulatory apparatus, new games often make their debut in Atlantic City. There also is always a good mix of denominations, from nickels right up through five dollars. (Penny multiline games are just beginning to appear there.)

My favorite places to play in Atlantic City are Bally's and Caesars, but I like most of the casinos. Starting at the west end of the Boardwalk (Absecon Island, on which Atlantic City sits, faces southeast into the Atlantic Ocean, so the Boardwalk runs east to west), we find the Atlantic City Hilton—formerly the Grand, formerly the Golden Nugget. This last "formerly" is why I like to visit and stay at the Hilton. Steve Wynn designed the place right, and after all these years the classy white-on-gold motif survives. It is a lovely place, with a rather smallish casino that is stocked with the best of the new games, particularly dollar reel-spinners. More space would allow the selection to be better, but it would ruin the atmosphere. Keep it like it is.

If it's selection you like, no place is better than the Atlantic City Tropicana. We talked before about the wacky promotions they run at this casino, but the slot floor itself is huge, and is divided into all these themed areas featuring different kinds of games. You'll find everything your heart desires here, from multiline video to classic reels to special in-house bonus games like the Fortune Dome, where the slots dispense tickets that you collect to redeem for a session inside a huge Plexiglas dome suspended from the ceiling. You get a minute inside the dome as thousands of dollars in cash swirl through, propelled by air, and you grab as many bills as your greedy little hands can snatch.

I always have fun at the Trop, like the time I played tic-tac-toe with the chicken, losing miserably, only to have my human team spirit lifted later in the evening when I was *dealt* a royal flush on a video poker machine. (I couldn't believe my eyes.)

Trump Plaza used to be on the lower end in terms of game selection, but for the past few years they have been knocking out walls and consolidating coin redemption booths so as to stuff in as many new games as possible. Nowadays, the selection is great. (You video poker enthusiasts out there, by the way, will find the city's only 10/7 Double Bonus Poker game at the Plaza.) Inside, the Plaza is like a throwback to the classic Vegas-style casino—dark and elegant, with fancy chandeliers over a central table game pit. It's a good "casino scene," which is why Brad Pitt met George Clooney there in the remake of *Oceans Eleven*.

My favorite night at Trump Plaza happened a few years ago, when it was still attached to the Trump World's Fair Casino. World's Fair is now a patch of dirt adjacent to Convention Hall, but it used to be my favorite casino. Donald Trump bought it after the two former owners failed to make a go of it. It was created as the Playboy Casino Hotel, which closed after Hugh Hefner failed to get a license and its subsequent owner, Elsinore, quickly realized that a multilevel, James Bond–style casino was not generating much excitement among the elderly bus patrons. ("*Chemin de fer*? Never heard of it. Where's the buffet, sonny?") A redesign into something called the "Atlantis" didn't fare much better. But Trump revamped the facility the right way— he took out all the table games, filled the ground floor with nickel slots, and put in good video poker. Ironically, the reason I loved playing at the World's Fair is the same reason it does not exist anymore— it never got really crowded.

Anyway, I was playing a slot at the World's Fair one night when I hit a thousand-dollar jackpot. Now, as I advised earlier, a big jackpot like that should always be a cash-out event. So, naturally, I kept playing. But now I was in the mood to party. I started ordering Crown Royal on the rocks, and, because of the lack of crowds, cocktail service was always prompt. I ended up getting totally snookered before staggering back over to the main Trump Plaza casino hotel, where my room was. My wallet was stuffed with cash, so I decided to play a little blackjack at the Plaza on my way to bed. I remember sitting down at the table. The next thing I remember is waking up in my room the next morning. Cringing with fear, I reached for my wallet to see if it was empty. Every bill I left World's Fair with was there, except for my hundred-dollar buy-in at the blackjack table. "Whew, only lost a hundred dollars," I thought, but then I looked at the nightstand and saw a huge stack of five-dollar chips. It turns out I had won about *four hundred dollars* at that blackjack table, evidently while totally unconscious.

Hey, it doesn't get any better than that.

East of Trump Plaza is the start of the center-Boardwalk string of Caesars Entertainment properties—Caesars Atlantic City, the Wild Wild West annex to Bally's, Bally's Atlantic City, and the Claridge, which is now called the Claridge Tower at Bally's. Caesars is my favorite place to stay on the Boardwalk, but for pure playing I'll stay in any one of these four places. They are all connected inside, forming a massive complex of casinos with thousands and thousands of slots of all stripes. You can truly find anything you want in the way of slot machines in these properties. Even the "Claridge Tower" has great game selection nowadays.

I used to go the Claridge all the time when it was just the Claridge, because it had the best collection of quarter 9/6 Jacks or Better video poker in the city (it's the easiest strategy to learn, so I was able to do okay). But what they never had there were any new slots—they typically had to stretch every dollar just to keep the place open. When Caesars Entertainment took over, the first order of business was to start buying every new slot machine that came down the road. They took out the good video poker, but they replaced it with what is now one of the more enviable collections of multiline video slot games in town.

Back when the Claridge was threadbare and in constant financial turmoil, I made a joke in a column that its motto was "At Least We're Not the Sands." I still feel this way about the hotel at the Sands (next door to the Claridge), which is crying mournfully for a facelift. The Claridge is more than 70 years old, and its hotel is in much better repair than the 20-year-old Sands. There is new hope for the Sands, though. They recently did a renovation and added a great nightspot called "Swingers," playing up the Rat Pack theme of the now-gone Vegas hotel that gave the property its name. (The Sands still pays the owners of the legendary Vegas Sands to use the name and logo, by the way.) There is a new emphasis on poker, and they're putting back many of the table games they removed recently. The Sands has always had one of the best selections of new slot games in town, often beating out the other casinos as the debut location of new games. Hopefully, they will now do something about the hotel.

Before you get to the "eastern bloc" of Boardwalk casinos—Resorts, Trump Taj Mahal, and Showboat—stop at New York Avenue and the Boardwalk, at the Ripley's Believe It or Not! Museum. For ten dollars, you get to view artifacts and films making up some of the weirdest oddities of Ripley's famous collection. ("Marvin Flemstone, the Human Arm. Believe it or not.") Then it's on to Resorts, which has improved its slot floor exponentially over the past few years. It is now one of my favorite spots, and what's even cooler, I recently found out the place is haunted. I was told by a Resorts official that the hotel, the former Chalfonte-Haddon Hall, was converted into a military hospital during World War II, and many of the dead GIs from the basement morgue are still there. And they're getting comped, too.

Trump Taj Mahal is matched only by the Trop in the enormous number of slot machines it offers its customers. The Taj is huge—a football field full of all kinds of slots, from reel to video. The hotel rooms also are among the best in town. The place is massive. They even have benches at strategic locations on hotel floors to rest during what becomes a crosstown journey from the front desk to your room. It's like walking through the hotel in *The Shining*. And all this space is decked out in that gaudy, ornate style that typifies the Donald. (It is Trump's monument to himself.) The Taj also has one of the best slot clubs in town, with same-day cash back and constant sweepstakes giveaways.

Showboat, with its Mardi Gras theme, great restaurants, and beautiful hotel, is an excellent place to stay. But, to play, skip down to Resorts. The problem is that, since Harrah's Entertainment took over Showboat, payback percentages have gone the way of the old bowling center that used to be on the property. And forget about video poker—it's horrible here.

Over in the Marina district, it's pretty much the same thing with the payback percentages at Showboat's sister property, Harrah's Atlantic City, although the hotel itself is one of the best places to stay in town. Harrah's just put in a new tower that turned it into the closest thing to a Las Vegas mega-resort in the city. (Until Borgata opened, anyway.) Harrah's also has one of the best selections of new games in town, and was the first casino in Atlantic City to extend the slot floor all the way to the hotel lobby. But, again, the payback—particularly in video poker—leaves much to be desired.

Maybe it's just sour grapes on my part; in the 17-odd years I've been going to Atlantic City as of this writing, I have never personally walked out of Harrah's a winner. It's not that jackpots are absent at Harrah's—lots and lots of people win there every day, just not me. Of course, they love me. Harrah's stock goes up three points every time I walk in the door.

Next, we have another one of my favorites, Trump Marina. I number this place among my favorites not for the slot floor, which has a game selection not nearly as good as at Harrah's or Bally's or Trop or Taj or several other spots in town. But the place has some of the coolest slot club promotions around, like shooting dice for a million bucks. I also love the Marina's hip atmosphere and the cavalcade of rock acts it brings to its showrooms and lounges.

I know, I know. It's a slot book, and again I'm allowing my obsession with rock music to dictate my recommendation for a place to play. Fact is, I'd go to Trump Marina even if the place had *no* slots. Where else can you see Roger Daltrey, Sting, Prince, Alice Cooper, the Goo Goo Dolls, David Lee Roth, and Meat Loaf at the same place, in a single year? The Marina was the first place in Atlantic City to move beyond acts like Steve and Eydie, Tony Bennett, and Paul Anka to bring in the performers of my "g-g-generation." That's why I go there.

Finally, we have the newest casino in Atlantic City, the Borgata. This is a place you absolutely must see, particularly if you like the big Vegas mega-resorts. It is like a merging of the elegance of a place like Bellagio with the hipness of Mandalay Bay. You'll find some of the best nightspots, restaurants, and hotel rooms in town here, and the slot floor offers remarkable selection in multiline video, and a surprisingly large inventory of full-pay video poker games. Personally, I love the oldest casinos in Atlantic City, but the Borgata represents the first glimpse of the New Atlantic City. It has raised the bar on quality, and the older resorts are still busy renovating and making additions to catch up—which is good for everyone.

Before we move on to slots elsewhere in the country, one more Trump story (most of my Atlantic City road stories involve Trump in some way): I play in a blues band called Voodoo Weasel (yes, "Voodoo Weasel"), and we did a gig a few years ago out on the deck at Trump Marina. It happened to be Donald Trump's birthday, and my friend Larry Mullin, who was the property's marketing VP at the time, brought the Donald out to hear us. He arrived just as we were playing J. Geils Band's "First I Look at the Purse." He thought we were busting on him.

We were never asked back. But I still play slots there, because I usually win at Trump properties. In fact, several major appliances in my house are courtesy of Mr. Trump, having been purchased after I hit sizable jackpots.

Thank you, Mr. Trump. When it comes to slots, first I look at *your* purse.

Chapter 14

Tales from the Road: The South

There is a region of the country where, since the early 1990s, slots have blossomed like a magnolia tree on the grounds of an antebellum mansion, where the bars and cherries on slot reels proliferate faster than the stars and bars on the local flag, where video bonus rounds draw casino patrons like boll weevils drawn to a cotton field in the searing Delta sun.

(Sorry. I just had an attack of Simile.)

Yes, I am speaking of "the South," that part of the country once known as "the Confederacy," a name still favored by many of its residents. Casinos first came to the South on August 1, 1992, when the Isle of Capri opened its temporary facility in Biloxi, Mississippi. Today, slots can be found at dockside, riverboat, and land-based casinos in Mississippi, Missouri, and Louisiana (pronounced "Loozanna"); Indian casinos in North Carolina and New Mexico (pronounced "New Mexico"); and gaming cruise ships sailing from Georgia, Florida, and South Carolina.

Unlike during our visit to Atlantic City, when I told you a bit about each and every casino, I'm going to concentrate on a few casinos in each Southern location to give you the flavor of what it is like when "y'all go playin' slots dahn theyah." In fact, because so many casinos are spread out across the country these days, the rest of our road trips will give you highlights of the offerings rather than the kind of exhaustive, laborious thesis I provided on Atlantic City or Las Vegas. This is partly because my trips to Southern locations have been on an occasional rather than constant basis (I'm always in Vegas or Atlantic City), and partly because I am a lazy, shiftless, no-account slacker.

Our first stop in the South is North Carolina, home of Andy and Opie and Aunt Bee and Barney Fife and Floyd the Barber, where the state slogan is, "Tobacco Is a Vegetable." There is only one casino in North Carolina, managed by Harrah's for the Eastern Band of Cherokee Indians. Called Harrah's Cherokee Casino, it is nestled in the Smoky Mountains of western North Carolina, a beautiful casino replete with fountains, mountain foliage, rock formations, and hillbillies.

Slots at Harrah's Cherokee are unlike those anywhere else in the nation, because of North Carolina's gaming law. Only video games are permitted, and the law requires all of them to have an element of skill. When the casino opened, all the games were video poker, video blackjack, and video craps. Casino officials, though, asked slot-maker IGT to figure out a way they could offer video versions of the most popular IGT reel-spinners and still meet the state's skill requirement. IGT engineers put their noggins together and came up with something called "Lock-n-Roll," a series of IGT video slots that are just like the manufacturer's top reel-spinning games, such as Double Diamond, Wild Cherry, and Red, White, and Blue, except they all have a "re-spin" feature. With each reel result, the player has the option to "lock" any or all of the reels, and re-spin any remaining reels to achieve a new result.

It is much like the "draw" feature in video poker. The "skill" involved is looking at the pay table and judging whether there is a good chance of improving a reel result, or deciding it is best to keep the result of the spin as-is. All right, it's not exactly "skill" like brain surgery or raccoon hunting, but it was enough to satisfy the North Carolina authorities.

Payback percentages on these games still average out to returns comparable to those in Atlantic City—anywhere from 83 percent to 98 percent. However, after playing these Lock-n-Roll games for a while, you can develop strategies for winning and slice the house edge down quite a bit.

Or, you can just go to Mississippi.

When you go to Mississippi, you will find casinos that, in their slot offerings, are not much different from Atlantic City. The payback percentages, in fact, are a point or two higher than New Jersey overall (in 2002, the three casino regions in Mississippi turned in overall paybacks close to 94 percent, compared to Atlantic City's 92 percent), and the mix of games is very similar, since Mississippi modeled its regulatory apparatus after that of New Jersey.

However, while the slot offerings are similar to Atlantic City, the hotel employees who serve you in Mississippi, and the fellow players you encounter, are quite different.

Picture Atlantic City in slow motion, and with a Southern drawl. Everyone you meet is always "fixin'" to do something. As in, "Jasper's fixin' to whip up some grits and throw hotcakes on the griddle." Or, "I'm fixin' to whomp on your Yankee hide." In the setting of a casino resort, this laid-back, Southern demeanor always translates into that legendary "Southern hospitality," with employees fixin' to satisfy your every need. But it also translates into "slow." It used to drive hyper Northerners crazy when the first resorts opened in Biloxi. It often took 45 minutes to get your car out of valet parking, because all the attendants were always "fixin' to mosey on down" and "git" (or sometimes "fetch") the next customer's vehicle.

I'm sure part of it is because of the weather, which in Mississippi is so humid from May through September that you can't go outdoors without feeling like a wet sock in a drawer full of molasses. Take five steps in the July heat and humidity and you are overcome by an urge to whittle. It's true. You just want to put on overalls, stick a shaft of wheat between your teeth, "set down" on a front porch, or a curb, or under a big ol' tree, and "commence to whittlin'." I'm sure few of the wooden structures in Mississippi were created through traditional construction methods. They were all whittled.

After gaming was legalized in Mississippi in 1990, the first casinos were paddlewheel-style riverboats that looked like the old gambling boats that cruised the Mississippi River in the 19th century, and in *Maverick*. But soon someone realized that the law required only that casino boats be placed floating in a navigable waterway, and that barges do just that. So, in one of the most ingenious developments ever devised to skirt the intent of a gaming law, operators simply linked anchored barges together to form a flat surface on the water, and built land-style casinos on top of them.

Thus, the larger casinos in Mississippi are, by and large, indistinguishable from land-based casinos, except that they have water underneath them. Going in the front door of one of these "dockside" facilities, one does not feel like one is going on a boat. It seems just like any other casino. If a barge ever slipped loose from its moorings and floated out to sea, you would have slot players strolling out the front door unaware and dropping like shark bait.

Driving into Mississippi from Tennessee (Hey, that sounds like a country song!), the first casino jurisdiction we encounter is Tunica, just down the river from Memphis. Before casinos were legalized, Tunica's civic motto was, "Just Down the River from Memphis." Tunica itself was one of the poorest counties in Mississippi, a place where Saturday night meant grabbing an extra pickle from the barrel at the general store.

Dockside casinos completely reversed Tunica's fortunes, which is to say they *created* Tunica's fortunes. Operators like Caesars Entertainment (when they were the separate Bally's and Grand Casinos), Boyd Gaming, Harrah's, and Horseshoe Gaming built fabulous dockside resorts that were as nice as anything on land, and Tunica's casino center prospered to the point that today the nine casino resorts in Tunica constitute the third-largest gaming jurisdiction in the nation.

Grand Casino Tunica is the largest resort in town. It is, in fact, the largest non-Indian resort between Atlantic City and Las Vegas, with a total of 140,000 square feet of casino space spread across four themed areas. The slot floor is massive, and is packed with just about every kind of slot game you can imagine. If it's the "resort experience" you seek, check out either this place or Sam's Town, another massive casino, or Horseshoe, with its all-suite hotel, or the Hollywood, with its cool collection of movie memorabilia.

As usual, though, I go for the smaller joints: Fitzgeralds, where drinking is as it should be—in an Irish pub—or the Sheraton, which crams the best slots in the business into its small casino.

There are several casino jurisdictions spread across Mississippi; Natchez and Lula are the closest ones to Tunica, and then you have paddlewheel riverboats in Vicksburg, along with some great historic Civil War stuff—but from Tunica I prefer to head straight down Highway 55, through the heart of Delta blues country (where I can stop and pay homage to my many dead blues heroes), to the Gulf Coast, where Biloxi and Gulfport are separated by a coastal highway dotted with dockside casino resorts.

Driving to Biloxi through blues country is much more fun than flying there. If you fly, it's a good bet you'll get routed through Atlanta, where you will board one of those little propeller planes. I always feel like I should be wearing a parachute on these things. The cockpit is divided from the cabin by a little curtain, so you can hear the pilot say things like "Oh, my God!" Even if he's only spilled some coffee or something, you think the plane's going down. I don't know about you, but if I were going to crash I would prefer it to be with a hundred tons of steel surrounding me, not a bunch of metal panels bolted together like Legos.

The Gulfport-Biloxi airport has been growing every year, but it's still pretty teeny. And if you do fly there make sure you rent a car, because there are roughly three taxicabs in the entire region. They don't sit waiting at the airport like in Vegas, either. If you want a cab, you ask a guy downstairs to call one for you. "Sarah, git me the taxi company. Some Yankee city-folk's in town, goin' to the *Ho*-tel."

Okay, I'm exaggerating, but it really was like this in Biloxi as recently as 1997 or 1998. The first time I went there, we had the guy call us a cab and what arrived was a 1976 Chevy Impala in need of a ring job, driven by a guy named "Cooter." He was fixin' to get his cab repaired, he told us on the way, ever since he "done broke down in Mobile." The locals credit casino mogul Steve Wynn with bringing more taxicabs to the area. Steve couldn't find a cab one day, so he did what anybody would do: he started a cab company. By the time he opened his new resort, the Beau Rivage (French for "Where the hell are the taxis?"), you could finally find a cab when you needed one.

The Beau Rivage, an MGM Mirage resort, is the cream of the Gulf Coast market. There are lots of good places to play down here, including both Grand Biloxi and Grand Gulfport for great resort amenities; Treasure Bay and Isle of Capri for fun themed environments; and the President for great fishing and an excellent golf course. But none even come close to the Beau for a Vegas-style luxury resort experience. (And, yes, it's another one of my "lucky" places as well. One night, it was both lucky *and* unlucky, when I won a ton of money on quarter slots and gave it right back on the dollar slots. Big-shot slot expert, right?)

But, just as in Vegas, for pure slot playing go where the locals go. I like to head for the Back Bay area, to the New Palace and the Imperial Palace, because they have great payback percentages, good video poker, and a relaxed atmosphere away from the hustle and bustle of the coastal highway.

One night, when I was staying at Grand Biloxi (or maybe it was Grand Gulfport; they're interchangeable) with several of my coworkers from *Casino Player,* our meeting times got screwed up and they ended up going over to Treasure Bay without me. (You *Player* folks reading this already know the story I'm going to tell, because you've told it to others a million times, thank you very much.) Left to my own devices, I did what anyone would do—found a bar, played bar slots, and got completely hammered drinking . . . you guessed it, Crown Royal. It was a repeat of my Trump Plaza performance, except this time I didn't win.

At two in the morning, my friends came back from Treasure Bay, found me at the bar just as I was about to go back to my room and collapse, and dragged me to the poker room. I sat down in a chair, and then, instantly, it was the next day in my hotel room. (Funny how that happens sometimes.) My pants were all scrunched up in a corner of the room, and in the pocket was a gaming chip that read, simply, "NO PLAYER." It had evidently been placed in front of my lifeless carcass as I sat at the poker table the night before. I am told, amid considerable chuckles, that my friend Maureen placed all my bets for me that night as I sat there like a mannequin. Eventually, they all figured I'd better get up to my room, so my "friends" guided my zombie-like hulk of a body out into the casino, pointed it toward the escalator, and cheerfully went back to playing poker. At this point, there were three possibilities for the remainder of my evening: end up sleeping in a decorative fountain, walk out the front door and keep walking until I reached New Orleans (or the Gulf shoreline, depending on the wind), or somehow manage to find my room. To this day, I have no idea how I arrived at the latter.

But, anyway, on to our next Southern state, Louisiana, and more specifically, New Orleans. (Pronounced "Naah'lins.") Most of the casinos anywhere near Naah'lins—or in Baton Rouge or in central Louisiana in general—are riverboat casinos, and, for reasons I will explain later when we visit the Midwest, I hate riverboat casinos. (I do have a few exceptions, which I will also explain.) When in Louisiana, I usually go to one of the three Indian casinos, Cypress Bayou Casino in Charenton, Paragon in Marksville, or my favorite, Grand Casino Coushatta in Kinder. This latter casino is the largest in the state, with a huge slot floor including more than three thousand machines and enough variety to satisfy any tastes.

Or I go to Naah'lins, because that's where Harrah's is. Harrah's Casino New Orleans is a gorgeous place, with 2,500 slots spread across five different themed areas, so I never run out of mul-tiline video choices, and I never become bored playing. But the real reason I go there is that it is smack in the heart of New Orleans, where the city's battle cry can always be heard: "Gentlemen, raise your glasses. Ladies, raise your T-shirts."

Where else can you go to a casino, play slots, and then go down the street to listen to absolutely the best jazz music you'll find anywhere, and then stop on the way out of town at some "fonky" voodoo shop to pick up a mojo hand?

Payback percentages, by the way, are around the same in Louisiana as they are in Mississippi. Same thing with Missouri, although I rarely play there, because of the silly rules—they track your buy-ins and the tokens and chips you draw during two-hour periods called "cruises" (even though the casino vessels don't cruise), because no one's allowed to lose more than five hundred dollars in a two-hour period. For the life of me, I can't understand why losing two thousand dollars in eight hours is any better, or why, in a single minute over the two-hour mark, it's okay to lose a thousand dollars instead of five hundred. (For the record, I prefer not to lose anything.)

There are nice places to play in Missouri, though. There are dockside barge casinos in St. Louis—Harrah's and President—but most of the Missouri casinos are riverboats. One of the only river-boats I actually enjoy playing in is a Missouri boat, the Argosy Casino in Riverside. While a paddlewheel-style riverboat (it remains docked on the Missouri River), it has one of the largest riverboat interiors I've ever seen. The game selection is so-so, but the size of the facility makes it unlike a lot of riverboats, and the restaurants are great. Not surprisingly, Argosy offers the highest payback percent-age in Missouri.

If we've gotten to Missouri, we're at the top of the South (and actually, out of the Confederacy, since Missouri never seceded from the Union). Or maybe we're at the bottom of the North, or the side of the Midwest, or . . . Oh, never mind! Let's get out of here!

Chapter 15

Tales from the Road: The North

It wasn't all that long ago that if a Northerner wanted to play a slot machine in his backyard he had to go to an illegal casino. Or buy a slot machine and put it in his backyard.

No more. The spread of casino gaming across the country has resulted in real, live, legal casinos spread across the Yankee domain, from New York to Detroit to Chicago to South Dakota to Canada. So pack up your long johns, my friends. It's time to hit the North!

You will definitely need the long johns on our first stop—the state of New York. The new slot palace there is, of course, the Seneca Niagara Casino, which the Seneca Nation Indian tribe opened on New Year's Eve 2002 on the U.S. side of Niagara Falls. For local businesses, the Seneca property, New York's first full-blown, Vegas-style casino resort, provides Americans with the long-awaited opportunity to look across the border to Canada's Casino Niagara and say, "*Nyaa*-nyaa!"

Seneca Niagara Casino was packed from the start. Thousands of gamblers waited in the rain on New Year's Eve to get in the door, almost starting a riot when the opening was delayed waiting for Governor George Pataki to get there. He never arrived, and they finally opened the place up after the crowd went and got the burger-meister and started lighting up torches.

The place has a nice selection of 2,625 slots, and the design is remarkable, considering the casino is in a converted aircraft hangar.

There will soon be casinos opening up in the Catskills (complete with Henny Youngman, I hope), but for now the Seneca casino joins one other full-blown slot spot in New York, the Oneida Nation's Turning Stone Casino in Verona, up in the Adirondacks. Turning Stone is a unique place, in that it is the first casino in the nation with a completely cash-free slot floor. The machines have no bill acceptors or coin hoppers. You go to the cage, sign your name, and get a debit card which doubles as a player's club card. Once you have your card, you can make deposits on it at the cage, or go to one of the employees who wander around with cart-style units to accept deposits. Once your card is loaded with money, you put it in the machine and a video keypad pops up on the screen for you to enter your PIN. Then, you play as long as you want. Winnings go to the account, or you play until you use up the deposit, and then go cash out the card at the cage or give them more money to load it up again.

I love this system, except for the Oneida Nation's "cure" for the complaints they got from customers that the place was too quiet. You guessed it—they added coin sound effects. They're more realistic than the jingly sound made by ticket-printing slots, but in this instance they made the coin-clanging sound *way too loud,* apparently to simulate the sound of some sort of giant mutant platinum coins hitting an enormous metal hopper tray right next to your ear. It's like someone has placed a bucket over your head and started hitting it with a hammer. After a few hours of this, though, the problem is all cleared up, because by that time you've gone deaf.

One cool thing about Turning Stone is that the gambling age there is 18 (not to worry—no alcohol is served), so in 2003 I was able to introduce my elder son, Joe, to the world of casino gambling. (Hey, it's a poignant moment in any father's life, isn't it?) The night I took him up there, I was absolutely on fire; it seemed I couldn't lose. The problem was that Joe couldn't win. I kept having to stop playing, take my card to the cage and cash some of it out to give my son more gambling money. Kids, huh?

Now for what's bad about Turning Stone: the game selection is putrid. They have these Atari-like video poker machines that they designed in-house, evidently back in the 1970s, and they buy regular slot machines from exactly two vendors: Sigma and Konami. No IGT, no Bally, no WMS, no Aristocrat . . . just three or four games from each of those two manufacturers. The other bad thing is the hotel room rate—$110 for a weeknight stay in an unremarkable room at a hotel firmly in the middle of nowhere.

Oh, and of course the old long johns came in handy. It was late April, and we woke up to freezing temperatures and a windy snowstorm. *New York, **Neew York!***

A much better choice for slot play up north is Connecticut, and its two middle-of-nowhere casinos, Foxwoods and Mohegan Sun. The opening of these two Indian casinos was another classic example of ingenuity in skirting the intent of a gaming law. The Indian Gaming Regulatory Act of 1988 gave Indian tribes the right to operate any game otherwise permitted under state law, so Connecticut's tribes used the state's "Las Vegas Nights" law, designed to allow churches to run card games to raise money, as the legal basis for opening full-blown casinos. (Connecticut lawmakers have just repealed the law, but the casinos stay. And because those two casinos stay legal the state's going to have a hard time telling other tribes they can't open casinos under the federal IGRA law.)

Foxwoods, owned by the Mashantucket Pequot Indian tribe, opened in 1992—before slot machines were permitted. It was an enormous, gorgeous roomful of table games in the middle of the woods of Ledyard, Connecticut. A year later, the tribe made a deal with Connecticut's governor, and got the exclusive right to offer slot machines in exchange for giving the state an annual payment of one hundred million dollars or 25 percent of the gross. The rest, as they say, is history—Foxwoods is now the most profitable gaming operation in the United States.

Hot on its heels is Connecticut's other tribal casino, Mohegan Sun, opened in 1996 down the deer trail from Ledyard in Uncasville. The Mohegan tribe cut a similar deal with Connecticut, and with the Pequots—who agreed to share their exclusive right to operate slots in exchange for getting their annual state payment lowered to $80 million.

Getting to these casinos is not a matter of a quick drive from the airport. They are deep in the wilderness. From the nearest airport, you'll need a rental car (preferably four-wheel drive), and it may be a good idea to have a dogsled at the ready.

But if you can get there without being eaten by wolves you will be blown away by the casinos. Both of these places are massive. Foxwoods has the largest casino in the world—more than 300,000 square feet. You could fit three Atlantic City casinos inside it. Mohegan Sun offers another 180,000 square feet of casino space—a two-Atlantic-City-casino capacity. As you can imagine, you will find every kind of slot machine you could ever want to play at either one of these casinos, with average payback percentages right around the same as Atlantic City. With five thousand machines at Foxwoods alone, if you can't find something you like here, well, your standards are weirdly high.

It's time to hop a few states over to Michigan, and the urban casinos of Detroit. There are three of them there: the MGM, Greektown, and MotorCity. All are run-of-the-mill, Atlantic City–style casinos with run-of-the-mill, Atlantic City–style payback percentages.

They also are all temporary facilities. The operators were supposed to open permanent facilities by 2000, but the city was unable to secure the riverfront land to put them where they wanted. All three are now planning permanent facilities elsewhere in the city. Greektown plans to crowd development onto seven acres downtown. MotorCity owner Mandalay Resort Group is planning a 17-story hotel with blue-tinted reflective glass, aluminum trim, and neon, with heavy use of signage and what it calls "super graphics," on 25 acres off the Lodge Freeway. MGM plans a new sandstone-colored casino downtown with bronze-tinted glass, with a central "illuminated water-steam-ice sculpture." Huh? Water, steam, and ice? It seems that what they're saying is that this thing is going to melt at some point. (Maybe it's just me.)

Playing slots at any of these casinos is sort of like playing slots in Atlantic City, except that you have to pay for your drinks, and they stop serving alcohol when the Detroit bars close at 2 A.M. (A good or a bad thing, depending on your perspective.)

In general, playing slots in Detroit is both good and bad. It's good, because the casinos are in Detroit, where there are great pro sports, fantastic bars and music nightclubs, theater, and other nearby activities you'd expect in a Northern city. It's bad only because that Northern city happens to be Detroit, and if you stray too far from the heart of the casino district you may find yourself in the heart of the chalk-outline district.

There is one more casino in the Detroit area—Casino Windsor, across the river in Windsor, Ontario. As I once noted in a column, something about Windsor makes it seem like a foreign country, but that's only because it *is* a foreign country. It is Canada, which is rumored to be outside of the United States. Therefore, you will be paid in funny-looking Canadian money, in bills bearing a picture that is either the Queen of England or Martha Raye. I can't really tell. The nautical-themed Casino Windsor is a huge place, with lots of good variety in multiline video and reel-spinning slots, but with lousy video poker.

When you head back over the bridge to the U.S., your car will be scrutinized carefully. Not for explosives, but for Cuban cigars. This always seems to be the most pressing concern of the border guards—illicit tobacco. Oh, and not many of these border guards are really intimidating. The last one I encountered looked like he'd just gotten back from the senior prom. He had pimples, and I think his name was "Skippy."

There are a bunch of Indian casinos in Michigan also—16, to be exact. Most are smallish, with snack-bar-style restaurants, small hotels, and limited game selection on the slot floors. One exception, at least as far as game selection and casino size, is Chip-In's Island Resort in Harris. The casino there is huge, around 135,000 square feet, with loads of slot selection and a good slot club with great promotions. But, as with the Connecticut casinos, if you go in winter you'll need a dogsled, or one of those snow tractors like they had in *The Shining*.

From Michigan, we go over to the Chicago area—or, as they call the region in the casino business, "Chicagoland." Chicagoland casinos consist of several gaming riverboats either anchored or sailing in or around Lake Michigan. These are really the kinds of casinos I want to describe in the Midwest chapter—you know, the ones I don't like. So we'll revisit Chicagoland along with the Midwest slot palaces.

Other northern casinos of note can be found in Deadwood, South Dakota. These places are really cool. What they did was to take the Old West mining town of Deadwood, nestled in the Black Hills, and transform all the historic buildings into little casinos. Each casino license is limited to 30 slot machines, so don't expect selection—but, *man*, you've got to see this place anyway. All of the buildings in which they placed slots, poker, and blackjack operations are required to conform to Deadwood's historic architecture, which means the town still looks like it did in the 1880s, when Wild Bill Hickock got shot in the back of the head there holding aces and eights, forever thereafter known as the "Dead Man's Hand." Wild Bill and Calamity Jane are both buried in Deadwood.

In fact, the No. 10 Saloon, where Wild Bill was shot, is now one of Deadwood's casinos. You can gamble in the spot where he met his end. How cool is *that*?

One other kind-of-northern spot that I didn't mention back when we stopped in Las Vegas is the Reno/Tahoe area in Northern Nevada. Reno is kind of a small town disguised as a city, and the casinos there and in the suburb of Sparks are much like the locals casinos in Las Vegas—good percentages, great video poker, friendly atmospheres. If you want to go resort-style, check out the Eldorado and Silver Legacy downtown. But for my money the best spot for slot play in Reno is the Atlantis, out by the airport. Here, you will find some of the best paybacks in town, plus a great slot club with good cash back and fantastic promotions.

While you're in the area, you've got to check out Lake Tahoe. This is one of the most beautiful spots on the planet, with gorgeous resorts on the lake like Harrah's and Caesars, and one must-see—the Cal-Neva, Sinatra's old joint. One can almost feel the ghosts of Frank, Dean, Sammy, and Momo Giancana. Also of interest at the Cal-Neva: the lodge room where you can get your picture taken standing right on the California-Nevada border.

"Now I'm in California. Now I'm in Nevada. California. Nevada. California. Nevada. . . ."

As we have traveled across the northern part of the country, we have skimmed over the borders of the next region we will visit on our journey, the Midwest. So it's on to the cornfields and the riverboats.

But first, one more time: California . . . Nevada . . . California. . . .

Okay, I'm ready. Let's move on.

Chapter 16

Tales from the Road:
The Midwest

The Midwest. The Heartland. The Breadbasket of the World. Home to cornfields, basketball teams, all-American family values, right-wing militiamen, and, of course, casinos.

Actually, the Midwest—Iowa in particular—was the site of the first casino operation outside of Nevada and New Jersey. It was here, in Bettendorf, that Bernard Goldstein launched the first riverboat casinos in the nation, when he started the company that would eventually become Isle of Capri. On April 1, 1991, Goldstein threw open the gangplanks to the *Diamond Lady* in Bettendorf and the *Emerald Lady* in nearby Dubuque—replicas of 19th century steam-powered Mississippi paddlewheel riverboats, each with small casinos on board. He soon had plenty of competition, and today there are 12 casino riverboats in Iowa, 10 boats in Indiana, 4 in Illinois.

This is why I rarely play slots in the Midwest. By and large, I hate riverboat casinos. Oh, I have to give them their due for the money and employment they have pumped into local Midwest economies, and I write about them in my trade journal and in the player magazines to which I contribute. But that doesn't mean I have to like them. After all, this is *my* book, you know.

For someone like me, who has spent 20 years playing slots in real-life, Vegas-style resort casinos, the riverboat experience just doesn't cut it. Let me tell you about the first time I visited a riverboat casino. To get there, I had to drive a rental car through these neighborhoods that looked sort of like Berlin in 1945, only with rap music, with town mottoes such as "The Spent Shell-Casing Capital of the World." I got to the "land-side pavilion" of the riverboat casino on an "off time," which is to say between cruises. So I had to wait an hour for the next cruise. But here's the thing: *The boat was sitting right there the whole time.* It was "permanently docked." This is a riverboat term that means the state in which the riverboat casino is located has exempted that boat, or all boats in the state, from the requirement it actually cruise on water.

Some states have relaxed cruising requirements permanently for all boats, simply because cruising requirements do not make sense. They were initially imposed, as I explained a few years ago in one of my *Strictly Slots* columns, to prevent the monstrous vice of gambling from polluting the morals of the people in the crack houses of the surrounding neighborhoods. But the way the laws were written many operators could satisfy the cruise requirement by digging a little canal and having their vessels float back and forth in about 10 feet of water, like a toy boat in a bathtub. So some states permanently discarded the cruise requirement. Other states, such as Missouri, permit casino vessels to remain docked when casino officials alert them of dangerous conditions in the water, such as a candy wrapper on the dock.

But the problem is that, even when states have relaxed the requirement that boats actually cruise, they haven't changed the rules about cruising *schedules,* so casino vessels must still have "boarding times" for "virtual cruises." In other words, you must pretend that you're cruising. You have to wait in line to get on the boat at a specific boarding time for your pretend cruise, and once you're on you can't get off and get right back on—you have to pretend to swim to shore and wait for the next boarding time.

In addition to all this silliness, for someone who has been going to Vegas-style casinos for 20 years, getting on most riverboat casinos is like walking into your closet with two dozen of your friends. A lot of these places seem like someone stuffed slots, table games, and bars into a mobile home. You are so close to the next player that you can count his nose hairs.

All that said, there are a few Midwest riverboats I do like. One is Caesars Indiana. It is a beautiful hotel attached to a huge riverboat casino, with a multitude of game choices and good video poker. Of course, to get there you have to drive through miles and miles of nothing. The last time I drove there, at one point I thought I heard the banjo music from *Deliverance.*

I like a few other riverboat casinos, like the Argosy boat I described in the South chapter, but by and large: thanks but no thanks.

Some land-based Indian casinos are scattered throughout the Midwest. There are some huge Indian casinos in Minnesota that I like, and even a couple of smaller ones in Kansas. If you go to the ones in Kansas, though, be prepared for a long drive across miles and miles and miles of cornfields, and then some more miles of cornfields. In Kansas, driving time is measured in dog years:

"Look at the horizon! Another field!"

"What horizon?"

Once you get to the western edge of the Midwest, you reach Colorado, where a small group of really cool casinos is nestled up in the Rockies, in Black Hawk and Central City. These towns have a lot of the little storefront casinos like you find in Deadwood, but also two nice, big casinos with lots of great game selection—Isle of Capri and Central City Station.

As more and more states look at legalizing some form of slot machine gambling as a way to address gaping budget deficits, there will be more places in the Midwest and other parts of the country to play slots, and this is likely to happen very soon.

But beware: many of these new slot locations are likely to be of the "racino" variety, meaning slot machines added to racetracks. To find out what's wrong with this type of slot facility, turn to our next chapter.

But, first, I have to tell you how to get to the Indian casinos in Kansas: Drive three hours, turn left at the feed store, and take a quick right at the manure pile. And make sure you have four-wheel drive.

Chapter 17

Tales from the Road: Racinos

During the past few years, a new kind of "roadhouse" has emerged to speckle the casino universe like a leaky oil pan speckles a driveway. It is identified by a hip new 21st century kind of nickname: "racino." A racino is a racetrack to which has been added a roomful of slot machines, making it a racetrack with a casino. So it's a "racino," get it? Isn't that clever?

Racinos came about because owners of racetracks, where people place bets as horses and dogs run around in circles (although usually not at the same time), began to peer into their grandstands on any given day and see the same three 80-year-old men, sitting amid roving bands of pigeons. In some locations, the three old men were clearly in danger of being overtaken by the pigeons, who became emboldened and rebellious due to their growing numbers, and began wearing leather jackets and smoking cigarettes.

As the pigeon-to-customer ratio got worse, it began to dawn on track owners that pigeons rarely actually bet on horses. With fewer bets, the purses for jockeys became smaller and smaller, until at some locations the jockey's prize for winning a race was that he got to eat the horse.

Then, in 1995, tracks in Iowa and in Delaware (where I happen to live at this moment) installed slot machines, and started to absolutely rake in the loot. Suddenly, track owners had to deal with curious carbon-based organisms that infested their entire properties. The organisms, long absent from the tracks, were referred to by a long-forgotten word in the racing business: "customers."

People in neighborhoods surrounding the racetracks, who suddenly realized they were 10 minutes away from slot machines, converged on the facilities like hungry dogs surrounding a piece of horse meat. They could play slots practically in their backyards—and, boy, did they ever. It didn't matter how much preparation or professional gaming-business expertise was employed in setting up the racinos. The tracks could have stuck slots in steaming piles of horse manure and people would have strapped on boots and flocked to play them. Overnight, racetracks that had been gurgling a raspy death rattle sprang back to life. States raked in money, and purses became huge, drawing the best thoroughbreds in the country. It didn't even matter anymore if there were only two people in the grandstands, because with slots the house was a-rockin' anyway. (Don't bother knockin'.)

One would think racinos attract mainly people who would have otherwise gone to Atlantic City, Vegas, or Mississippi to play slots. But if you go to a racino you can expect to see many more people who had never been inside a casino anywhere, until someone put one at the track. Oh, by the way—in most racinos, the house knows this too. Indeed, the house counts on it. That's why a racino is usually the absolute *worst place in the world* to go to play slots. The game selection stinks beyond stench, there's no video poker, there's no cash back, and you usually have to (Gasp!) pay for your drinks. There is only one possible reason any smart, discerning slot player would go and play slots in a racino: there's nothing else available.

If you do have another option, take it. Drive the extra hour to Atlantic City, or the extra four hours to Mississippi. Or take a cheap flight to Vegas. But if you're sitting there in Podunk, and your biggest excitement traditionally has been the semimonthly visit to Home Depot, then I understand that playing slot machines down the street can look pretty cool, and that you want to go to a casino and play slots after a five-minute drive instead of a two-hour drive or a five-hour flight.

The racinos understand this too, and, again, they count on it. That's the prime directive of the racino slot business: there's nothing else available.

"Hampershire Equestrian Park and Racino. Because Nothing Else Is Available."

And before you write me those nasty letters, racino owners, don't get me wrong; I'm not talking about service, or the quality of your facility, or your restaurants, or your concierge and valet parking attendants. I'm talkin' *gamblin'*. If it is slot machine or video poker gambling I seek, I would appreciate the liberal percentages, good pay schedules, comps, and cash back that I have come to expect. As it is now, why on Earth would I come to your joint instead of going to Atlantic City?

Many of the racinos have made their properties appealing, even luxurious. A few have added grand, exquisite hotels and restaurants. I stayed in rooms at Dover Downs in Delaware and Mountaineer in West Virginia that were larger than apartments I've had, and I've eaten in restaurants at racinos that were as good as anything in the non-horse slot market. (Or is it the "extra-equestrian" slot market?) But I have yet to see a racino slot floor that actually makes me want to go in and play.

The problem is that many of these places are run by bureaucrats from the state lottery. When it came time to add slots to tracks in the mid-1990s, some state officials just called lottery suppliers, because they already had them on contract, and asked for video lottery terminals. They bought them, put them in, and guess what? They're *still there*. Unlike in competitive markets such as Atlantic City, refreshing the slot floor with the latest games was never a priority at the racinos, because people were still playing the games that were there—not because they particularly liked them, but because that's what was there. It was a radical approach to slot management: success through stagnation, thanks to the racino's best pal, a captive audience.

When they do buy new games, it's not a matter of a slot manager picking up a phone and calling a slot manufacturer. To buy a slot machine, racinos often have to go through bureaucratic red tape such as requests for proposals, competitive bids, forms in triplicate, acts of Congress, white papers, black papers, court orders, search warrants, and DNA testing. By the time all the approvals are complete, the new game they are putting on the floor is old enough to vote.

Oh, and forget about "branded themes" or anything else that requires the casino to pay extra money for a game with a popular license. No *Wheel of Fortune*, no *Jeopardy!*, no Austin Powers, no Wink Martindale. (No Wink? Say it ain't so!) Just good old-fashioned slot machines that mostly look the same.

Consequently, playing slots in a racino is sometimes like entering a time warp and traveling to whatever year they added slots to the track. I can go to Dover Downs or Delaware Park and some of the games make me think I'm back in the mid-'90s, listening to Nirvana and wondering whether O.J. will be convicted. I even found Piggy Bankin' at Dover Downs recently, a game that came out back when I had hair. (Well, *more* hair, anyway.)

If a racino is your only option for slot play, at least you can comfort yourself with the knowledge that most of them offer payback percentages around the same level as Atlantic City or Mississippi. And, if you like reel-spinners, you'll find games that are just as updated as the games you find in real casinos, since reel-spinners are, by and large, the same now as they were in 1995. As for me, I like variety in my slots, and I like playing video poker. If a racino does have video poker, it will be one or two games, and they'll have pay tables that fall under the technical category of "suck," with a house edge that will assure the house makes money and you don't.

Of course, since I go to *all* casinos, not just casinos that are unattached to racetracks, I have developed favorites within the subdivision of gaming known as the racino. My two favorites are Dover Downs in Delaware and Mountaineer in West Virginia. As for Dover Downs, it's a place where I can drive an hour to stay in a hotel room that's as nice as anything Steve Wynn has ever offered. (Of course, if I *really* feel like playing slots and crashing in something comfortable, I'm more likely to go to Caesars Atlantic City, where they have 50-cent and dollar 9/6 Jacks or Better video poker, and I can smoke while I play them.)

As for Mountaineer, I like going there for two reasons. First, they just built a gorgeous hotel, relieving visitors of the need to stay in the "lodge," which is basically the Bates Motel with mountains. Second, it is in Chester, West Virginia, which is right outside of Pittsburgh. It is my native land. I can kibbutz with a lot of fellow Pittsburghers there. It's the only racino in the nation at which one can hear, and even use, the term "yinz" when talking to more than one person (as in, "Yinz are from Sahthside, huh?"), or ask for a chipped ham sandwich with a glass of pop and have them know what you're talking about.

While I may not particularly like a lot of the places, some of my most colorful road tales come from racinos. That's because they are unique among slot venues. It's fun to see how a "casino" is created by people who know nothing about casinos. My buddy Bob works in a racino, and I've been to Bob's racino lots of times. The first week he worked there, a guy dropped dead at his machine, and Bob's instructions were to proceed with casino operations as if nothing out of the ordinary was afoot. The incident was nearly seamless to slot operations, which continued as they continue any day, except for the fact there was a fresh cadaver lying in the aisle. "Here's your jackpot, sir. Congratulations! Oh, him? He died about an hour ago. What's that? No, don't worry. That snorting sound always happens when rigor mortis sets in."

Once, a dead pigeon fell from the ceiling of Bob's racino into the lap of a lady playing a slot machine. The structure that housed the slot casino had been built decades earlier, and apparently some of the pigeon population had become stuck in the rafters.

The woman, of course, reacted as if a bloody corpse had fallen into her lap, evidently failing to see the humor in the situation. I'm sure she bears long-term emotional scars from the tragedy, with nightmares in which she's stuck in a Hitchcock movie with dead birds falling on her in the Wal-Mart.

And the pigeon? I'm afraid he was DOA. Attempts to resuscitate him were useless. He was sent to the kitchen with his fellow casualties, and there was soon a new dish at the buffet called "Poultry Surprise."

As for the people you meet in your average racino, they range anywhere from your "Average Joe" looking for a "Good Time" to your "Average Homicidal Maniac" looking for "Fresh Meat to Rip Apart with a Meat Cleaver." Don't expect the kind of (ahem) sophisticated, highbrow crowds you see in Vegas or Atlantic City. You see, a lot of these racinos were built in areas where there were a lot of biker bars, and, judging from my own experiences, probably a couple of institutions for the criminally insane.

Tales from the road? These are more like Tales from the Crypt.

At one racino that is close to my home, which I will not identify by name except to say that it is one of three racinos in Delaware, they traditionally had state police present whenever the slots were turned on. From the mid-1990s until 2002, if there was trouble at this unnamed racino, there were always a couple of state troopers there who could, in the parlance of law enforcement administration, "crack some skulls."

Recently, budget considerations—brought on by the smoking ban called the "Indoor Clean Air Act," also known as the "Economic Suicide Law"—caused this unnamed racino to suspend the services of the off-duty Delaware State Troopers. The effect was quite similar to that of the U.S. Army's sudden removal of the Republican Guard from Baghdad.

I was there the first night there were no state troopers. A guy accidentally knocked over a woman's drink, and her boyfriend demanded he buy her another one. He refused, and the boyfriend took a swing at him and missed—but hit his own girlfriend square on the jaw, knocking her out cold on the floor. What followed was a pathetic spectacle of two guys rolling around on a fancy carpet while security guards stood there and said, "I'm not gettin' into *that*. Not for seven bucks an hour."

At this same racino, I was quietly playing a slot machine one night when a woman beside me went into some sort of psychotic fit. Apparently "hopped up" after a bit of "chemical refreshment," she wailed and flopped to the floor, where she began crawling around on her hands and knees and going, "Meeeo*www!*" like a cat. I thought she was going to cough up a fur-ball. Concerned security guards surrounded her and watched intently as she kicked and flailed and squirmed around on the floor like Curly from the Three Stooges. She was finally restrained and removed from the premises (before she could say "Ticonderoga"). It was a floorshow that would have made Wayne Newton jealous.

I have been to some racinos at which one would need to pool the resources of several women to create a complete set of teeth. I have seen guys whose physiques obviously required very little time in the gym, with flopping bellies stuffed into their flannel shirts (which, remarkably, are worn year-round), as the air filled with the sweet aroma of stale beer-breath.

These were, of course, isolated incidents, and isolated shady characters. Most people you see in racinos are normal, law-abiding, God-fearing Americans.

Which means things can get even scarier.

Chapter 18

The Modern
Slot Jockey

The characteristics of slot players described in the preceding "road" chapters are symptomatic of a group of humans to whom I like to refer collectively as "the modern slot jockey." This particular subculture of human, like any subculture, displays an inspiring mix of sociological characteristics that distinguishes its members from the general population.

Oh, sorry. For a second I thought I was writing a college term paper. Damn flashbacks. Let's just say most slot jockeys are a lot alike. Although some are different. But all of them are a lot different from slot jockeys of 30, 20, or even 10 years ago. The nature of the slot jockey has changed with each major change in slot machine technology. Before the 1960s, the slot jockey was usually a woman waiting for her husband to finish shooting craps or playing blackjack. With the introduction of the game Money Honey in 1964, slots started to look much more interesting than they had. Before Money Honey, a slot machine was usually a big metal box with a handle and three windows for the reels. Suddenly, they had lights and noises that began to attract a new kind of follower known as the "Guy." At the time, the typical Guy in a casino was a World War II veteran, rollin' dem bones just like he had on a ship somewhere in the Pacific. Whether they were doing that or playing cards, they were gamblers.

Now remember, in the 1960s slots were never thought of as anything but a gambling box. "Entertainment" had no place on a slot floor, or anywhere else inside the casino. If you wanted entertainment, you went to the showroom to see Sinatra or Sammy. If you went into the casino, you went to gamble.

Consequently, when members of the group known as Guys joined the slot jockey subculture, they brought the "gambler mentality" with them. Plus, they brought cigars and chewing tobacco and stuff like that.

When dollar slots, with big hoppers that *clanged* dollar tokens into a metal tray, began appearing everywhere in the 1970s, the sound of money attracted more Guys, who gravitated toward the slot floor like zombies who had just been summoned by their grim master. This influx changed the nature of slot jockey culture even more— now, it included lots of Guys who just wanted to sit down and, as they liked to put it, "win some damn money." So now, when you looked at a slot floor, all the games were lit up and making sounds, but the players were not. A row of slot players behaved much in the same manner as a row of factory workers, each screwing a bolt on something as it passed on an assembly line. They would pull and grunt and pull and drink and pull and chew.

You see, once the novelty of the lit-up, electromechanical Bally slots wore off, the games were, in the end, electrical versions of the mechanical slots. Men and women alike just sat there pumping coins, pulling handles and watching reels spin. It was about as exciting as reading a telephone book.

But that was okay, because we were all there to gamble! And gambling is serious business. By the late 1980s, though, the ranks of serious slot jockey gamblers had been infiltrated by normal humans, people who wanted excitement from their gambling experience— even (gasp!) *entertainment*. Slots were still traditional, but they now had huge jackpots, and double-jackpot wild symbols, and red, white, and blue blazing 7s times two, and stuff. Big jackpots and lots of coins in trays made slots look like fun—not only to the hardcore gamblers, but to Irving Finkerhouse, the insurance salesman from Pittsburgh. (Irving will get you a good deal on term life, by the way.)

With all sorts of normal humans now wandering around the slot floor, the character of the slot jockey began to change again. The fate of the subculture would be sealed, however, when the riverboat and Indian casinos sprang up in the early '90s. Suddenly, traveling to Nevada or Atlantic City was no longer a prerequisite for being a slot jockey. Normal humans who had jobs and kids and lives were now treating a trip to a casino like bowling night. As slots became more entertaining, and even *funny*, Middle Americans from all walks of life became slot jockeys.

What this all means is that modern slot-jockey culture is a mixture of your Everyman or Everywoman with crotchety old traditionalists like me who still like to spin for the gold, and don't mind watching reels spin for, like, a week at a time. However, within the diverse ranks of the modern slot jockey are several groups with similar characteristics, so we can do maybe a teeny little sociological study on them.

The largest divisions are, of course, male slot jockeys and female slot jockeys. The differences between these two groups, and the interaction between them, are a fascinating study in itself.

Guys still have that old gambling instinct when they play slots, which is to say they approach the game as if it were a sport: "I'm 10 bucks down, with three yards to go." They keep score as they play. Even if they're watching something as preposterous as a cartoon of Wimpy eating a hamburger, they keep one eye on that credit meter. That's the scoreboard. It's a contest. "Only 10 credits left. I'm gettin' my ass kicked!" If a guy scores a big jackpot, the experience is identical to watching one's team (that would be the Steelers) intercept the ball and run 90 yards for a touchdown. The fist goes pumping in the air. You let out a guttural, barely human growl or shout "Yessss!" like Marv Albert after a slam-dunk.

Girls, we *live* for that feeling. Jackpot! Slam-dunk! Yessss!

Winning is an intoxicating thing. That's why I never believe anybody who says a casino is intentionally trying to prevent people from winning. Casinos need winners, especially guy winners. The notion that you can score a touchdown is what keeps guys going back to that ATM after they lose. You figure you may have lost, but it's only halftime. The ATM is like the coach's pep talk. "Here's another hundred! Now get out there and fight! It ain't over till it's over!" Then, of course, it's over.

When women play slots—especially video slots—they don't necessarily watch the score. They don't relate the second level of a bonus round to having a power hitter up with two men on base. They "experience" the game. They actually soak in the entertainment. They play—and I swear this is the truth—for "fun"!

Women will actually notice all the little nuances of the bonus game when they play a video slot. That's because they are there in the casino to have a "good time." Their reactions to winning and losing are totally different from a man's reaction. If they lose, they actually appreciate that they had a "good time" even if they did lose. "Oh, that was fun!" they'll say. A guy can laugh his head off at a bonus game and still want to gouge out his own eyes if he loses, possibly to sell them to get more gambling money. Women just chuckle it off. (And then go cheerfully to ask their husbands for more money.)

In fact, women are always cheery and perky when they play slots. They're even cheery and perky if someone else wins a progressive jackpot for which they have been pumping quarters into a machine for hours. "Oh, good for you!" they'll say. "It's great to see someone win!"

What? If someone else wins my progressive jackpot, I view him as a parasite who has just robbed me of everything I have worked for in my entire life. I even know how these machines work—that a jackpot is random, dumb luck, and it can happen to anybody at any time—and I still want to kick the guy in the spleen. Even though guys look at slot playing as a sport, "good sportsmanship" is rarely a consideration in this game. That crap is for golf. You won my jackpot, you crumb.

Female slot jockeys are also totally different from guys when it comes to winning. As I explained before, guys react to jackpots like they do to a touchdown, but in between the big jackpots they behave more like racecar drivers. The spin button is like the gearshift lever—we drive it, and start pressing harder to shift gears when reasonably sizable jackpots appear. The big hit is like the finish line. Yesss! On the other hand, if you lose, it's like getting a flat tire. You feel you have to go back to the pit and have your crew—which consists of your wallet and the bill acceptor—get you back into the race.

Women, on the other hand, tend to react to every tiny hit as if they had just won a refrigerator on *The Price Is Right*. "*Eeee!* Five coins!" "*Aaaaaggh!* Two cherries!" For bigger jackpots, these exclamations are often in the form of a shriek so loud it causes any man within a 50-yard radius to lose all bodily functions for an instant. If there are cops in the casino, they reach for the crime-scene tape. By the end of several hours sitting next to a woman having even moderate luck on the slots, your average guy can become a quivering mass of nerves, walking with a noticeable palsy-like shiver in all joints and jumping three feet in the air at any sound.

There's also the hunting-and-nesting thing that comes into play when you talk about male and female slot jockeys. Guys are always on the "hunt" for the next jackpot, even if they win. That's why casinos love us. Women, though, can actually exercise an attribute that is totally foreign to me and a lot of guys I know who play slots. I think they call it "common sense."

My wife, Karla, actually goes through a cognitive process after winning a jackpot. Instead of just shouting, *"Yeah-ahh!"* and continuing to play when a big hit happens—which to me is the perfectly natural and sensible thing to do—my wife will go through a remarkably quick calculation to determine, to the penny, the difference between her buy-in and the credits she has won. She then cashes out her credits, keeping the winnings for actual future use in purchasing goods and services, and puts her buy-in amount back in. It's an amazing thing to watch. I should take my checkbook to the casino and have Karla balance it just after she's hit a jackpot, because at that instant she's in the *zone* when it comes to math. I, on the other hand, wallow in a particularly male characteristic known as "greed" after hitting a big win:

"Gimme more. Gimme gimme gimme. Sure, I won a hundred bucks, but that was three seconds ago. What have you done for me lately?"

Other groups in the slot-jockey subculture are common to both sexes. I described many of these groups in the "jerk" chapter. They include Machine Abusers, Militant Anti-Smokers, Machine Hoggers, Chit-Chatters, Busybodies, Cowboys Who Scream "Yeehah," Advice-Givers, Know-It-Alls, Self-Absorbed Anti-Casino-Owner Crusaders, and the like. Then there are the Party Kids, those who always have a "good time," win or lose, and are amiable and happy any time they're in a casino. (We all hate them.) Some Party Kids also belong to the Hoodoo Voodoo group, those who perform exotic rituals to summon luck as they play.

And let's not forget the Sloshers. We've all been part of this group at one time or another. These are people who, during the course of an evening, forget just why it is that casinos offer free drinks to slot players. You see, right around the fourth bourbon and soda, the ability to reason departs right along with the consonants in your speech. What follows is the systematic depletion of your net worth, as you reach for your wallet, stagger to the ATM, and keep playing and playing.

"Another bourbon and soda?"

"Aaarrooahh-garrfleshmock."

"Here you go!"

"Grmmmiff."

If I'm settling in for a long session at the slots, I order a Coke. Consequently, I rarely wake up on an Atlantic City beach with vagrants going through my pockets. Unless I want to, that is.

Of course, there are always remnants of ancient slot jockey culture mixed in with the mass of modern slot jockeys. These are the people who still approach a slot machine as if they had a job to do, a military campaign with the objective of victory at all costs. "If we are not victorious, let no man come back alive!" (General George Patton, slot jockey.) These "serious" slot players tend to come out more in the wee hours of the morning, after all the normal humans have gone to sleep. They derive their pleasure only from winning. Entertainment is for schmucks, they think. Let's get in there and gamble!

Oftentimes I will infiltrate this class of modern slot jockey. It invariably happens when I begin playing video poker late in the evening. Video poker has not been covered in this book, because I am not a video poker expert. I am a video poker *student*. My GPA is still pretty low, but it is improving steadily. For anyone who has not played a video poker machine for hours on end, it is hard to consider five-card hands flashing on a screen as "entertainment." When you get into it, though, you get into something of a rhythm. A mesmerizing tap-dance with the devil. You play and play, and then you play some more. Before you know it, hours have passed and the entertainment-seekers have all left the casino, leaving you with your fellow serious slot jockeys and fellow video poker players, who all look like bleary-eyed, dog-faced soldiers at the end of a three-day march. You play like a man on a mission, tapping the button with grim determination, until you finally get the signal that it's time to quit.

That signal can come in one of two forms. Either you take your wallet out to get another bill and moths come flittering out, or you hear the clanking and clattering of attendants throwing boxes next to slot machines all around you.

That's the drop for the hard count. It means the sun's coming up. That means the only slot jockeys left on the floor are the hard-cores who don't mind playing while someone vacuums the rug around their sleep-deprived bodies.

For me, it's my signal that the "gaming day" is over. Give me a wake-up in, say, two hours. Like Sinatra said, "Sleep when you're dead." Of course, he was still alive when he said that. I'm pretty sure.

Chapter 19

It's Cool Being a Slot Expert

You know, reporters don't often fall into prize gigs like the casino beat, where "research" often involves intense journalistic exercises such as staying in a suite or ordering room service. Or playing slot machines. Or watching Sherman Hemsley on a casino stage dancing to that "Movin' On Up" song for the trillionth time.

More often than not, a reporter's research involves stuff like sitting at a school board meeting taking notes, or feigning interest while some city planner shows you blueprints of a new solid waste management system. ("It's a win-win!") At one point between jobs writing about casinos, I was in Washington covering Capitol Hill for an education newsletter, and that involved cool stuff like wearing big press tags emblazoned with "United States Senate, Press Galleries." What an icebreaker in the singles bars! Except, I was married by then and never got to try it out. (I can *dream*, can't I?)

Of course, pretty soon the novelty wore off from seeing how huge, bulbous, and beet-red Ted Kennedy looks in person—after that, covering education became a bit tiresome. I mean, how many stories can you write about federal education programs being plucked out of Reagan-era budgets like ticks being plucked off a dog?

I just recently read an article in *Newsweek* that reminded me of those days, and of how everything in life is somehow related. When I was covering education, I used to follow Reagan's education secretary Bill Bennett around Washington as he explained to various groups why it was better that the country develop new weapons than to pump money into education programs for our children, many of whom could not identify the United States, or for that matter the planet Earth, on a map. Bennett went on to become Reagan's "drug czar," and subsequently wrote books and lectured to express his ultraconservative views on society.

Well, now I find out from *Newsweek* that Bill Bennett is a *serious slot jockey!* He plays $500 reel-spinners, and video poker, and has $200,000 lines of credit at various casinos. My opinion of the man has completely changed; Bill is now okay in my book. The media have heralded reports of his losses, which they say have totaled eight million dollars over the past decade, and he snaps back that he has won as much as he has lost—overall, he's even, and he has no gambling debt, and he doesn't use grocery money, or federal education dollars, to gamble.

You tell 'em, Billy Boy! Don't take any crap from those anti-gaming nimrods!

Anyway, I always wrote freelance about slots, but I did take one more detour in my full-time career, this time into the corporate world. I was a "Writer of Briefs." Betraying my union roots like a ratfink sellout, I worked for a time on the management side of labor relations at Conrail, writing briefs for "the Company" in labor disputes going to arbitration. On a more basic level, what this meant was that I was a writer who worked for a lawyer. I would write something like, "He broke the rules," and it would come back, "He violated the *burpus probandis* of the prevailing *corpus latchem delecti* notwithstanding the foregoing."

As you can imagine, I was happy to get back to being a full-time casino writer and slot expert. It always was a cool gig. Back in the '80s, there were still a lot of executives left who had served the wiseguys in the old days, so you would always get the royal treatment when you came into town to write about them. Once, my wife and I were picked up at the airport by a limo and taken to a casino hotel, where there was a suite with champagne waiting. Well, okay, it was an airport van, and it was a regular hotel room with wine coolers in a vending machine. But the point is, people thought we were high rollers, when in truth we had about 70 bucks on us. It was because "the Boss" invited us. And I don't mean Springsteen, either. In between interviews with the chief executive of the casino, we were treated to anything we wanted in the hotel—whether we wanted a soak in the Jacuzzi, a spa treatment, a gourmet dinner, or to have someone whacked.

No, I made up the last one. Like I said before, this was after DeNiro and Pesci had already been kicked out of the Tangiers.

The corporate types running the casinos these days don't spread out the red carpet quite as much, but this gig is still a blast. It's' even a blast when you go to stuffy professional industry events. Every year, I've gone to trade shows—which are perfect opportunities to network with one's colleagues in the casino business. And to eat like a big fat pig and drink yourself into a stupor. I even like moderating seminars, which are designed to permit attendees to sleep off hangovers while men in suits drone on with the enthusiasm of a doctor describing a gallbladder procedure.

Since I've been writing extensively for player magazines, though, one of my main activities has been playing slot machines. And then writing about them. And then playing some more, and writing some more. And this is considered "work." Is this a great country, or what? Among the many side benefits has been the acquisition of inspiring tidbits of specialized knowledge, such as what it feels like to win a jackpot while unconscious from alcohol consumption, or how to discern the viscosity of bread pudding in a casino buffet.

And then, of course, I get to go on radio and TV and explain to microphones and cameras what an RNG does in a slot machine. I have learned that my own voice, which, as I speak, sounds to me like that of a he-man professional news anchor, transforms when broadcast over airwaves into the voice of Jerry Lewis as the Nutty Professor. I have also learned how to be a talking head on television—how a half-hour taped interview can be edited into three sound bites displayed amid scenes of slot jockeys pullin' dem handles, and how a long statement such as, "I once ate through a $20 bill at a slot machine in a minute, because I was lost in the bonus game, which played the song 'Pop Goes the Weasel,'" can be edited down into a sound bite of me saying, "I ate the weasel," in a Jerry-Lewis, Nutty-Professor kind of voice.

Another cool part about being a slot expert is what becomes known to you as "business travel." Traveling is always a hassle, and always induces, at some point in the journey, the notion that you would rather be dead, rotting beneath the ground in a stinking box, than in your current location. But in this business you never get saddled with a trip to, say, Fargo, North Dakota, in February for a board meeting, or to meet with some client at the Holiday Inn in Scranton, Pennsylvania. You may get tired of airports, but you're always going to Vegas, or the Gulf Coast, or Central City, Colorado. Okay, it can also be Detroit or St. Louis or Chester, West Virginia, but even then you're going to a cool place once you get there. Well, cooler than other places in Detroit or St. Louis or Chester, anyway.

The writing itself is even cool, mainly because the entire history of the subject matter is fraught with coolness. I feel bad for writers who must trace the history of subject matter such as medical technology or logging equipment. No I don't, because they probably make more money than me. Still, as far as I know, neither the history of medical technology nor that of logging equipment includes San Francisco saloons and Chicago speakeasies and wiseguys and Senate hearings—or, for that matter, Popeye, Herman Munster, and the Amazing Spider-Man.

And, again, you can't beat the research procedures. Writing about slots is not bad work if you can get it, because it requires "playing." How many jobs require you to play?

It's not that I always have fun playing slots—sometimes I actually am "working," because I evaluate a lot of new slot games. And believe me, it can be dangerous work. Once, I dropped a quarter and it rolled on the carpet, and I had to bend all the way over to pick it up. I could have been killed!

When you see me at a slot and it looks like I am in deep concentration, I probably am—I am performing an on-the-spot calculation concerning the behavior of the slot in front of me, and discerning whether or not to recommend it to others in prose. But the cool part is that I'm still doing this work by playing a game with a chicken in it.

I also get to come in contact with a cavalcade of humans who work at all levels in the casino resorts. I'd like to take this opportunity to thank each of you individually for never throwing me out of your establishment. To the hotel desk clerks, thanks for sending people up to my room who actually know how to turn on the desk lamp.

To room service staffs, thank you for adding the terms "lukewarm" and "viscous" to my cache of responses to the question, "How do you like your steak?" To coin redemption cashiers, thank you for not speaking English. It just would have confused me anyway. To the cocktail servers on the slot floor, thanks to the lousy ones who showed up once or twice during the entire night, because I usually won when that happened. As for the efficient cocktail waitresses, well, let's just say you performed your duties in an exemplary manner, which means I don't remember any of you.

And to all my colleagues in the ranks of slot jockeys (Local 354), our little journey through the parallel universe of slot machine culture is just about coming to an end. It is time to hit the cash-out button of parenthetical attribution, scoop up the coins of simile, wipe off the grimy hands of alliteration and tip the washroom attendant handing you this pristine towel of modern literature.

What I mean to say is, the book's almost done and my wrists hurt and I'm running out of metaphors. So reserve my machine, put in my player's club card, and I'll see you out on the slot floor. Oh, and leave me some money at the cage.

Farewell, fellow slot jockeys! Victory will soon be ours! Ultimately, we shall win millions!

Or lose trying.

Acknowledgments

Upon completion of this book, I feel I have to step outside of my goofy, cartoon persona and express my appreciation to some of my fellow humans who made the work possible. First of all, thanks to Duane Burke for getting me into this most novel of industries. Duane, the publisher of *Public Gaming* and the late, great *Casino Gaming*, gave me the chance to get out of full-time freelance writing about city council meetings and landfills and into full-time gaming writing—and kept feeding me work writing about the industry long after I had left his company. Thanks to Roger Gros, my current boss and the main force in bringing me to *Casino Journal*, which enabled my long-term casino industry education to continue uninterrupted. Thanks to Paul Dworin, who gave me freelance work in between *Casino Gaming* and *Casino Journal*, and who kept me on my toes as my worthy competitor for so many years before most recently becoming my other boss and, along with Roger, giving me the leeway to finish research and writing on this project.

And big thanks go to Glenn and Adam Fine, who, for 10 years, gave me an invaluable forum in which to develop my expertise, between *Journal*, *Casino Player*, and, most of all, *Strictly Slots* and *Atlantic City Insider*, the two publications that gave me the opportunity to develop my current semipsychotic writing style.

Thanks to those in the industry who made this book possible as well. Thanks to Joe Kaminkow, Mickey Roemer, Julie Mottes, Marcus Prater, Jim Jackson, Kathleen McLaughlin-Harris, Dave Lyons, Kent Young, Laura Olson, Bob Bittman, Olaf Vancura, Mike Colaiaro, Mac Seelig, Jerry, Jeff and Jason Seelig, Alex Hartl, Brooke Dunn, Larry Pacey, and all my other slot-making buddies who gave me access to their inner sanctums over the years so I could continue writing about all the new slots. Thanks to Ali Saffari at IGT and Randy Adams from the former Anchor Gaming for all the tidbits of information imparted over the years on how slot machines work. Thanks to Frank Scoblete for making this book part of his popular

"Get the Edge" series, and thanks to Anthony Curtis, Jean Scott, Bob Dancer, Jeffrey Compton, and all the other gaming journalists for their constant support.

Special thanks to my lovely wife Karla, for putting up with my constant casino excursions and for not throwing my luggage on the front lawn after losing trips.

And, finally, thanks to all you slot jockeys out there, whose letters and questions over the years have constantly pushed me to seek out new information to hone my knowledge of the slot machine, who have laughed at all my cornball jokes, and who have had the common decency and mercy to part with a few shillings to buy the book.

I will try to repay you all. (The check's in the mail.)

Index

Aladdin (Las Vegas), 100
Anchor Games, 14–15, 63
Anderson, Louie, 67–68
Anka, Paul, 115
Anti-Smoking Crusaders from Hell (ASCH), 79
The Argosy Casino (Missouri), 123, 133
Aristocrat Leisure Industries, 15, 68, 127
Armani, 90
ASCH. *See* Anti-Smoking Crusaders from Hell
Atlantic City attractions
    boardwalk, 56, 105–8, 113
    gypsy fortunetellers, 108
    House of Knowledge, 108
    musicians, 108
    Ripley's Believe It or Not! Museum, 114
    rolling chairs, 108
    Swingers, 113
Atlantic City casinos
    Atlantic City Hilton Casino Hotel, 55
    Atlantic City Tropicana, 111
    Atlantis, 112
    Bally's Atlantic City, 105–6, 111, 113, 115
    Bally's Wild Wild West Casino, 109, 113
    Borgata, 106, 109–10, 114–15
    Caesars Atlantic City, 111, 113, 138
    Claridge Tower, 113
    Harrah's Atlantic City, 114–15
    Playboy Casino Hotel, 112
    Resorts International (Chalfonte-Haddon Hall), 105, 114
    Sands, 113
    Showboat, 114
    Trump Marina, 115

Trump Plaza, 106, 108, 112–13, 122
Trump Taj Mahal, 114–15
Trump World's Fair Casino, 112
Atlantic City developers
    Caesars Entertainment, 109
    Harrah's Entertainment, 114
    Park Place Entertainment, 108
    Trump, Donald, 112, 114–16
    Wynn, Steve, 111
Atlantic City entertainment, 115
Atlantic City Expressway, 106
Atlantic City Hilton Casino Hotel, 55
Atlantic City Insider, 71
Atlantic City locations
    Atlantic City Expressway, 106
    Marina district, 108, 115
    New York Avenue, 114
    Pacific Avenue, 110
The Atlantis
    Atlantic City, 112
    Reno/Tahoe, 130
Atronic, 69
Australian-style video slots, 16

Baccarat, 107
Baldwin, Alec, 85
Bally Manufacturing, 7
Bally's, 8–9, 12–13, 67–69, 127
    Atlantic City, 60, 105–6, 111, 113, 115
    Grand Casino Hotel, 55
    Las Vegas, 101–2
    Wild Wild West Casino, 109, 113
Bankroll, 29–30
Barbary Coast (Las Vegas), 90, 101–2
Beating slots. *See* Systems to beat slots
Beau Rivage (Mississippi), 121
Before *Wheel of Fortune* (BWOF), 63
Bellagio (Las Vegas), 90, 97, 101–2, 115
Bennett, Bill, 152
Bennett, Tony, 115

The Big Road (Las Vegas), 95
Binion's Horseshoe (Las Vegas), 91,
    99, 103
Blackjack, 26, 107, 112, 118, 129
Blazing 7s (slot game), 13, 29, 69, 144
Blue Diamond Road (Las Vegas), 90
Blue Diamond Saloon (Las Vegas), 90
Board games (slot themes), 63, 66–68
Boarding Pass program, 95
Boardwalk (Atlantic City), 56,
    105–8, 113
The Boardwalk (Las Vegas), 100
Boger, Bunky, 60
Bonanza, 69
Bonus games, 14, 16, 39–40, 66, 111
Borgata (Atlantic City), 106, 109–10,
    114–15
Boulder Highway (Las Vegas), 92
Boulder Station (Las Vegas), 89
Boulder Strip (Las Vegas), 97
Bourbon Street (Las Vegas), 90, 102
Boyd Gaming, 120
Brando, Marlon, 75, 79
Break the One-Armed Bandits
    (Scoblete), 52
Buffets, 57
The bus station (Las Vegas), 89
BWOF. *See* Before *Wheel of Fortune*

Caesars
    Atlantic City, 111, 113, 138
    Indiana, 133
    Las Vegas, 97, 101–2
    Reno/Tahoe, 130
Caesars Entertainment, 120
Cal-Neva (Reno/Tahoe), 130
Candy Land, 70
Captain's Club at Harrah's (Atlantic
    City), 55
Cartoon stars (slot themes), 66–67
Cash back, 57–58, 60, 137
Cash coupons, 56–57, 61
Cash Encounters (slot game), 68
Cash for Life (slot game), 67
Cash prizes, 61
Cash-out button, 58, 109, 155
Casino Center Boulevard (Las
    Vegas), 99
Casino Gambling Exposed (Gibbs), 53
Casino marketing department, 59

Casino Player, 20, 71, 122
Casino Windsor (Ontario), 129
Casinos. *See* "Racino"; *specific casinos*
Catskills, 74
CDS Gaming, 70
Central City Station (Colorado), 133
The Charles Nelson Reilly Show, 61
The Charo/Jimmy Walker "Dy-no-
    mite!" Revue, 61
Chickendales (slot game), 69
China Grill, Mandalay Bay, 98
Chip-In's Island Resort (Michigan), 129
The Chrysler Building, New
    York–New York, 100
Cigar stores, 3
Circus Circus (Las Vegas), 102
Clapton, Eric, 95
The Claridge/Claridge Tower
    (Atlantic City), 71, 113
Clooney, George, 112
Coast Casinos, 95
Colorado casinos
    Central City Station, 133
    Isle of Capri, 133
Comic books (slot themes), 66–67
Comic strips (slot themes), 66–67
Comps
    buffets, 57
    cash back, 57–58, 60, 137
    cash coupons, 56–57
    cash prizes, 61
    merchandise, 55, 57, 61
Compton, Jeffrey, 58
Connecticut casinos
    Foxwoods, 127–28
    Mohegan Sun, 127–28
Cooper, Alice, 115
Cooper, Gary, 83
Copperfield, David, 97
Corleone, Michael, 73
Corleone, Sonny, 73
Cosa Nostra, 73
Costner, Kevin, 73
Coupons runs, 57
Craps, 26, 118
Crazy Fruits (slot game), 69
Credit meter, 56
Credits, 59
CSI, 40, 86, 98
Cypress Bayou Casino (Louisiana), 123

Daltrey, Roger, 115
Dancer, Bob, 2
Dark Side of the Moon, 75
Delaware Park (Delaware), 138
DeNiro, Robert, 22, 153
Diamond Lady (Iowa), 131
Dig in the Desert, 60
Dirty Harry, 73
Dixon, Willie, 96
Double Diamond (slot game), 13, 29, 50, 118
Dover Downs (Delaware), 137–38
Downtown Las Vegas, 99
Dr. Moreau, 15
Duke, Patty, 44–45, 47

The Easter Bunny (myth), 33
Eastern Band of Cherokee Indians, 118
Eastwood, Clint, 73
Easy Street (slot game), 70
Eldorado (Reno/Tahoe), 130
Electro-mechanical, 8
Elsinore, 112
Emerald Lady (Iowa), 131
Eubanks, Bob, 67
Excalibur (Las Vegas), 99–100
Exhibits. *See* Touring exhibits

Family Feud (slot game), 67
Fey, Charles August, 3, 5–6
Fiesta Rancho (Las Vegas), 94
Fife, Barney, 72
Filthy Rich (slot game), 64
"First I Look at the Purse," 116
Fitzgeralds (Mississippi), 120
Five Times Pay (slot game), 13, 29
The Flamingo (Las Vegas), 7, 96, 101
Fortune Cookie (slot game), 69
Fortune Dome (slot game), 111
Foundation Room, Mandalay Bay, 97–98
Four Queens (Las Vegas), 99, 103
Foxwoods (Connecticut), 127–28
Freebies, 56
Fremont Downtown (Las Vegas), 99, 103
Fremont Street (Las Vegas), 90–91, 99

Gambling device, definition of, 1
Game chips, 35–37

Games of chance, 2
Games. *See* Slot games
Gaming riverboats, 15
    casino boats, 119
    "dockside," 120
    gambling boats, 119
    paddlewheel-style riverboats, 119
Gans, Danny, 97
Giancana, Sam, 61
Gibbs, Steve, 53–54
Glitter Gulch (Las Vegas), 90, 99
Golden Age of the Slot Theme, 66
Golden Nugget
    Atlantic City, 55
    Las Vegas, 90, 99
Goldstein, Bernard, 131
Goo Goo Dolls, 115
Gotham landmarks/Big Apple, New York–New York, 100
Grand Biloxi (Mississippi), 121–22
Grand Casino Coushatta (Louisiana), 123
Grand Casino Hotel (Atlantic City), 55
Grand Casino Tunica (Mississippi), 120
Grand Gulfport (Mississippi), 121–22
Great Depression, 7
Greektown (Michigan), 128
"Grim Reaper," 87
Gucci, 90
Gum vendors, 6–7
Gumball Machines: The Naked Truth (Legato), 1
Guy, Buddy, 97

Hard Rock Casino (Las Vegas), 95–96
Harrah's
    Atlantic City, 55, 114–15
    Captain's Club at Harrah's Atlantic City, 55, 57
    Cherokee Casino, North Carolina, 118
    Las Vegas, 60, 101
    Mississippi, 120
    Missouri, 123
    New Orleans, 123
    Reno/Tahoe, 130
Hefner, Hugh, 112
Henderson (Nevada), 93
Hendrix, Jimi, 95
Heston, Charlton, 74

High hit frequency, 20–22, 26, 29
  with low volatility, 22
High volatility, 21
High-paying machines, 38
High-rolling gamblers, 21
Hilton/Grand/Golden Nugget
    (Atlantic City), 111
Hit frequency, 19–20
Holiday Inn (Las Vegas), 89, 100
Hollywood (Mississippi), 120
Homeland Security (myth), 33
Hopper, 8, 51, 53, 58, 103, 109–10, 144
Hopper tray, 8
Hop-Sing, 69
Horseshoe (Mississippi), 120
Horseshoe Gaming, 120
Hot sauce (slot themes), 66
House of Blues, Mandalay Bay, 97
Howard, Moe, 93
Hughes, Skip, 2

IGT. *See* International Game
    Technology
Imperial Palace
  Las Vegas, 101
  Mississippi, 122
Indian casinos, 15, 123, 127, 129,
    133, 145
The Indian Gaming Regulatory Act of
    1988, 127
Indiana casino
  Caesars Indiana, 133
"Indoor Clean Air Act," 140
International Game Technology
    (IGT), 12–13, 63–65, 67–69, 73,
    93, 118, 127
Iowa casinos
  Diamond Lady, 131
  Emerald Lady, 131
Isle of Capri
  Colorado, 133
  Mississippi, 117

J. Geils Band, 116
"Jackpot fever," 12
Jackpot Party (slot game), 66
Jackpots, 6–9, 11–13, 17, 20–22, 28, 31,
    34–35, 37–38, 42, 47–50, 52, 59,
    139, 144–47
Jeopardy! (slot game), 65–66, 138

Jones, Jerry, 83

Kansas casinos, 33
Keep Your Hat On (slot game), 68
"Kin and cain't method," 29
King, B.B., 97
King, Don, 67
King, Larry, 67
King of Themes, 64
Konami, 127
Kramden, Ralph, 94

Lange, Jim, 67
Las Vegas attractions/promotions
  Beat the House seminar, 94
  castles, pirate ships, fountains, vol-
    canoes, 87
  Downtown casino center, 103
  drive-in wedding chapels, 103
  "family destinations," 88
  Fremont Street Experience, 90
  "full Vegas treatment," 87
  The Ghost Bar, 95
  "Las Vegas: What happens here,
    stays here," 88
  neon lights, flashy marquees, 87
  pool tables, 90
  seedy porno fliers, 88
  Slot-Jockey Heaven, 89
  "Space Needle," 103
  sports bar, 90
  Summit at the Sands, 96
  thrill rides, theme parks, 88
Las Vegas Boulevard, 96–97, 99
Las Vegas business, other than casinos
  CSI, filming of, 40, 86, 98
  Four Queens Parking Garage, 91
  In-N-Out-Burger, 89
  7-Eleven, 89
  Starbucks, 89
Las Vegas casinos, mega-resorts,
    89–90, 95, 97–102, 115
  Bally's Las Vegas, 101–2
  Barbary Coast, 90, 101–2
  Bellagio, 90, 97, 101–2, 115
  Caesars Palace, 97, 101–2
  Luxor, 98–99
  Mandalay Bay, 97–98, 100, 115
  MGM Grand, 97, 99–100
  The Mirage Resorts, 97, 100–101

Monte Carlo, 100
New York–New York, 97, 99–100
Paris Las Vegas, 90, 101
The Rio, 90, 95
Treasure Island, 101
The Venetian, 101–2
Las Vegas casinos, other than mega-
    resorts
  Aladdin, 100
  Binion's Horseshoe, 91, 99, 103
  The Boardwalk, 100
  Boulder Station, 89
  Bourbon Street, 90, 102
  The bus station, 89
  Circus Circus, 102
  Excalibur, 99–100
  Fiesta Rancho/Fiesta
      Station/Fiesta, 94
  The Flamingo, 96, 101
  Four Queens, 99, 103
  Fremont Downtown, 99, 103
  Golden Nugget, 90, 99
  Hard Rock Casino, 95–96
  Harrah's Casino, 101
  Holiday Inn, 89, 100
  Imperial Palace, 101
  Las Vegas Hilton, 102
  New Frontier, 102
  Orleans, 95
  The Palms, 95
  Riviera, 102
  Sahara, 102
  Sam's Town, 89, 91–93
  Santa Fe Station, 94
  The Silverton, 89–90
  The Stardust, 96–97, 102
  Stratosphere, 102–3
  Sunset Station, 89, 93–94, 98
  Texas Station, 89, 94
  The Tropicana, 99
  Westward Ho, 102
  Wynn Las Vegas, 102
Las Vegas developers, 86
Las Vegas Hilton, 102
Las Vegas, locals hangouts/suburbs
  Blue Diamond Saloon, 90
  Fremont Street, 90–91, 99
  Glitter Gulch, 90, 99
  Henderson, 93
  stinking little roadhouse casinos, 89

Las Vegas locations
  The Big Road, 95
  Blue Diamond Road, 90
  Boulder Highway, 92
  Boulder Strip, 97
  Casino Center Boulevard, 99
  Downtown Las Vegas, 99
  Fremont Street, 90–91, 99
  Las Vegas Boulevard, 96–97, 99
  Las Vegas Valley, 86
  The Mint, 90
  Mojave Desert, 98
  "New Four Corners," 99
  North Las Vegas, 97
  "Old Four Corners," 99
  Paradise Road, 95, 97
  The Strip, 92, 95–97, 99–101, 103
  Sunset Road, 97
  Tropicana/West Tropicana Avenue,
      95, 99–100
  West Flamingo, 95
Las Vegas, origin of name, 86
Las Vegas shows, 97
Las Vegas Valley, 86
LED screen/display, 64
Les Misérables, 16
Lewis, Jerry, 152
Little Green Men (slot game), 68
Little, Rich, 12, 65
Live-action video, 66
Lock-n-Roll (slot games), 118
LOSER, 27
Lost Continent of Atlantis (myth), 33
Louisiana casinos
  Cypress Bayou Casino, 123
  Grand Casino Coushatta, 123
  Harrah's Casino New Orleans, 123
  Paragon, 123
Low hit frequency, 21–22
  with high volatility, 22
Low risk, 21
Low volatility, 21–22
Lower-paying machines, 38
Luigi, 69
Luncheon meat (slot themes), 66
Luxor (Las Vegas), 98–99

Magazines (slot themes), 67–68
Mandalay Bay (Las Vegas), 97–98,
    100, 115

Mandalay Resort Group, 128
Marina district (Atlantic City),
    108, 115
Marketing department. *See* Casino
    marketing department
Martindale, Wink, 67, 138
Mashantucket Pequot Indian
    tribe, 127
McCarron International Airport, 89,
    91, 103
Meat Loaf, 115
Megabucks, 12, 65
MegaJackpots, 65
Merchandise, 55, 57, 61
MGM
    MGM Grand (Las Vegas), 67, 97,
        99–100
    The MGM (Michigan), 128
Michigan casinos
    Chip-In's Island Resort, 129
    Greektown, 128
    The MGM, 128
    MotorCity, 128
Mikohn, 28
Mills, Herbert, 6
The Mint (Las Vegas), 90
The Mirage Resort (Las Vegas), 97,
    100–101
Mississippi casinos
    Beau Rivage, 121
    Fitzgeralds, 120
    Grand Biloxi, 121–22
    Grand Casino Tunica, 120
    Grand Gulfport, 121–22
    Hollywood, 120
    Horseshoe, 120
    Imperial Palace, 122
    Isle of Capri, 117
    New Palace, 122
    The President, 121
    Sam's Town, 120
    Sheraton, 120
    Treasure Bay, 121–22
Missouri casinos
    The Argosy Casino, 123, 133
    Harrah's, 123
    President, 123
Mohegan Sun (Connecticut), 127–28
Mojave Desert (Las Vegas), 98
Monopoly (slot game), 28

Monte Carlo (Las Vegas), 100
Mötley Crüe, 56
MotorCity (Michigan), 128
Mountaineer (West Virginia), 137
Movie stars (slot themes), 63–67
Movies (slot themes), 63, 66
Mullin, Larry, 115
Multicoin, 8
Multiple-point days, 57
Myths, 33–45

"New Four Corners" (Las Vegas), 99
New Frontier (Las Vegas), 102
New Palace (Mississippi), 122
New York Avenue (Atlantic City), 114
New York casinos
    Oneida Nation's Turning Stone
        Casino, 126
    The Seneca Niagara Casino, 125
New York–New York (Las Vegas), 97,
    99–100
Newlywed Game (slot game), 67, 72–73
Newsweek, 152
Newton, Wayne, 2, 93, 97, 140
1960s–70s fads (slot themes), 66
Nitwit Jerks You Just Want to Punch.
    See Slotticus jerkus
No. 10 Saloon (South Dakota), 130
North Carolina casino
    Harrah's Cherokee Casino, 118
North Las Vegas, 97

Oceans Eleven, 7, 96, 112
"Old Four Corners" (Las Vegas), 99
Old Navy, 90
Olive Oyl, 82
One-armed bandit, 6–7, 14
Oneida Nation's Turning Stone Casino
    (New York), 126
Oprah, 30
Orleans (Las Vegas), 95

Pacific Avenue (Atlantic City), 110
The Palms (Las Vegas), 95
Paradise Road (Las Vegas), 95, 97
Paragon (Louisiana), 123
Paris Las Vegas, 90, 101
Park Place Entertainment, 108
The Patty Duke Show, 47
Payback chips, 35

Payback percentage, 19–20, 35–36, 38–40, 53, 59, 91, 94, 97, 102, 114, 118–19, 122–23, 128
Payout percentage, 36–37
Payout switch, 35
Pearly Gates (slot game), 69
"Perfectly Frank," 72
Pesci, Joe, 22, 153
Piggy Bankin' (slot game), 64, 138
Pinball machines, 8
Pitt, Brad, 112
Playboy Casino Hotel (Atlantic City), 112
Poker games
    bonus poker, 90–91, 95
    10/7 Double Bonus Poker game, 112
    video, 12, 16, 57, 81–82, 84, 90–91, 93–95, 98, 107, 111, 113–14, 118, 122, 126, 129–30, 137–38, 146, 148, 152
Poker hands/terms
    five-card poker, 2
    four Aces, 103
    four of a kind, 3
    "hitting the big one," 3
    inside straight flush, 82
    low pair, 82
    royal flush, 3, 111
    straights, 3
Poker machines, 2–3
Popeye (slot game), 67, 69
Potter, Harry, 48
The President
    Mississippi, 121
    Missouri, 123
Presley, Elvis
    jumpsuit display, 96
    slot themes, 63–65
Primitive video slots, 12
Prince, 96, 115
Prizes
    bonus money/coins, 14, 16
    bonus rounds, 14, 21–22, 27, 39, 66, 72–75, 117, 146
    cigars, 3
    drinks, 3
    "jack," 3–4
    jackpots, 6–9, 11–13, 17, 20–22, 28, 31, 34–35, 37–38, 42, 47–50, 52, 59, 139, 144–47

megabucks, 12, 65
"Pink Floyd Bonus," 75
"pot," 3–4
"reportable win," 3
10-coin payouts, 14
tokens for merchandise, 6
Twinkies, 75
Prohibition, 6–7
Promotions
    Bally Bowl, 60
    car giveaway, 58
    Cupid/arrow of love, 61
    Dig in the Desert, 60
    free rooms/show tickets, 61
    Game of LIFE, 60
    game shows, 60
    guess an eight-digit number, 61
    initial cash coupon, 61
    multiple points, 61
    multiple-point days, 57
    NFL winners, 60
    senior boxing competition, 61
    slot tournaments, 58–59
    sweepstakes, 58, 60
    tic-tac-toe with chickens, 59–60, 99, 154
    touring exhibits, 61–62
Puzzles (slot themes), 66–67

Queen of Comps. See Scott, Jean

"Racino," 133, 135–40
    Delaware Park, 138
    Dover Downs, Delaware, 137–38
    Mountaineer, West Virginia, 137
Random number generator program (RNG), 9–11, 16–17, 37, 39–44, 50, 153
Rat Pack, 7, 96, 113
Reagan, Ronald "Dutch," 152
Red Square, Mandalay Bay, 98
Redd, Si, 12
Reel-spinners, 3–5, 8–9, 12–16, 21, 28–30, 38, 40–41, 51–52, 64, 66, 90, 109, 111, 114, 118, 138, 144, 152. See also Telnaus virtual reel design
Reel symbols, 4, 6, 9, 15, 63
    bar, 6, 63, 123
    blanks, 9

Reel symbols (continued)
  fruit, 6, 63, 123
  high-paying symbols, 9
  low-paying symbols, 9
  multiplying wild symbols, 13, 63
  paying symbols, 13
  paylines, 15
  Red, White and Blue, 13–14, 118, 144
  same-colored symbols, 14
  7s, 63
  stops, 9
  wild symbols, 13, 22, 144
Reno/Tahoe casinos
  The Atlantis, 130
  Caesars, 130
  Cal-Neva, 130
  Eldorado, 130
  Harrah's, 130
  Silver Legacy, 130
Resorts International/Chalfonte-
    Haddon Hall, (Atlantic City),
    105, 114
The Rio (Las Vegas), 90, 95
Risqué Business (slot game), 69
Riverboat casinos. See Gaming
    riverboats
Riviera (Las Vegas), 102
RNG. See Random number generator
    program
Robison, John, 2
Rodeo, 83
Rooftop Diving Competition, 31
Rosenthal, Lefty, 96
Roth, David Lee, 115
Roulette wheels, 2, 14
"Rumjungle" club, Mandalay Bay, 98

Sahara (Las Vegas), 102
Sam's Town
  Las Vegas, 89, 91–93
  Mississippi, 120
Sands (Atlantic City), 113
Santa Claus (myth), 33
Santa Fe Station (Las Vegas), 94
Schultze, Gustav, 3
Scoblete, Frank, 52, 94
Scott, Jean (Queen of Comps), 57
Seneca Nation Indian Tribe, 125
The Seneca Niagara Casino (New
    York), 125

Sheraton (Mississippi), 120
Showboat (Atlantic City), 65, 114
Shuffle Master Gaming, 93
Sicilians, 73
Siegel, Bugsy, 7, 96, 101
Sigma Game, 69, 127
Silicon Gaming, 67–68
Silver Legacy (Reno/Tahoe), 130
The Silverton (Las Vegas), 89–90
Sinatra, Frank, 67, 130, 149
Slot club card, 41–42, 62, 155
Slot club promotions. See Promotions
Slot clubs/members, 55–57, 59,
    61–62, 95
The Slot Expert's Guide to Winning at
    Slots (Robison), 53
Slot games
  Blazing 7s, 13, 29, 69, 144
  bonus games, 14, 16, 39–40, 66, 111
  Cash Encounters, 68
  Cash for Life, 67
  Chickendales, 69
  Crazy Fruits, 69
  Diamond Line, 29
  Double Diamond, 13, 29, 50, 118
  Easy Street, 70
  Family Feud, 67
  Filthy Rich, 64
  Five Times Pay, 13, 29
  Fortune Dome, 111
  Fortune Cookie, 69
  "games within games," 14
  Jackpot Party, 66
  Jeopardy! 64, 138
  Keep Your Hat On, 68
  Little Green Men, 68
  Lock-n-Roll, 118
  Monopoly, 28
  Newlywed Game, 67, 72–73
  Pearly Gates, 69
  Piggy Bankin', 64, 138
  Popeye, 67, 69
  Risqué Business, 69
  South Park, 69
  Sphinx series, 69
  Ten Times Pay, 13, 29
  The Three Stooges, 67, 93–94, 140
  Throw the Dough, 69
  Trivial Pursuit, 28
  Wheel of Fortune, 15, 65, 138

Wheel of Gold, 14
Wild Cherry, 118
Slot Jockeys
  female slot jockeys, 145
  "gambler mentality," 144
  Hoodoo Voodoo group, 147
  "jerks," 147
  male slot jockeys, 145
  modern slot jockey, 143, 145, 147
  Party Kids, 147
  The Sloshers, 148
  slot jockey subculture, 144, 148
  See also Slotticus jerkus
Slot machine
  definition of, 1
  See also Board games; Cartoon
    stars; Comic books; Comic
    strips; Hot sauce; Luncheon
    meat; Magazines; Movie stars;
    Movies; 1960s–70s fads; Puzzles;
    Systems to beat slots; TV car-
    toons; TV commercials; TV
    game shows; TV sitcoms
Slot machine myths. See Myths
Slot machines (1803–Prohibition)
  Fey Liberty Bell, 7
  Liberty Bell, 5–6
  Mills Liberty Bell, 6
  My First Liberty Bell, 6
  "nickel-in-the-slot-machine," 2
  poker machines, 2–3
  three-reel design/contraption,
    3–7, 22
  wheel machines, 3
Slot machines (1941)
  Club Bell, 7
  console slot, 7
Slot machines (1964–2004)
  with arcade games, 15
  Bally's Wheel of Gold, 14–15
  Big Bertha, 79
  dollar machines, 8
  dollar-sized hopper, 8
  five-reel Big Win, 8
  Money Honey, 8, 143
  multiline video slots, 21–22, 26–29,
    38, 90, 95, 107, 111, 113
  Odyssey, space-age slot machine, 67
  with pinballs, 15
  six-coin, four-reel Continental, 8

video slots, 12, 14–15, 21–22, 26–29,
    38–39, 41, 59, 69, 93
Slot systems. See Systems to beat slots
Slot Theme Litigation, 15
Slot tournaments, 58–59
"Slots for Tots" controversy, 69–70
Slotticus jerkus
  Advice Givers (Slotticus jerkus
    knowitallus), 82
  Chit-Chatters (Slotticus jerkus
    diarrhea mouthicus), 81–82
  Cowpokes (Slotticus jerkus yeehah),
    83–84
  Machine Hogs (Slotticus jerkus
    swinicus), 80–81
  Machine Whackers (Slotticus jerkus
    abusus), 78–79
  Slot Panther Party (Slotticus jerkus
    militus), 84
  Smoke-Free Crusaders (Slotticus
    jerkus Everett Koopicus), 79–80
Smith, Anna Nicole, 74
South Dakota casino
  No. 10 Saloon, 130
South Park (slot game), 69
Sphinx series (slot games), 69
Spilotro, Tony the Ant, 96
The Stardust
  Atlantic City, 12
  Las Vegas, 96–97, 102
The Statue of Liberty, New York–New
    York, 100
Steve and Eydie, 105, 115
Stewart, Jimmy, 83
Sting, 115
Stinking little roadhouse casinos (Las
    Vegas), 89
The Stones (guitar display), 95
Stratosphere (Las Vegas), 102–3
Strictly Slots, 20, 71, 74, 79, 103, 132
The Strip (Las Vegas), 92, 95–97,
    99–101, 103
Sunset Road (Las Vegas), 97
Sunset Station (Las Vegas), 89,
    93–94, 98
Symbols. See Reel symbols
Systems to beat slots
  formula, 52
  "glitch," 49
  guaranteed system/method, 49

Systems to beat slots *(continued)*
   industry insider, 49
   inside trade secrets, 50
   insider information, 49, 51
   Internet sales pitch, 48
   magic system, 50–51
   ready to hit, 52
   secret system, 47–50, 52

Taj Mahal (Atlantic City), 61
Telnaus, Inge, 9, 11–12, 16, 40
Telnaus virtual reel design, 9, 11–12,
   16, 40, 51–52
Ten Times Pay (slot game), 13, 29
Texas Station (Las Vegas), 89, 94
"Theoretical worth" as player, 56
3-D graphics, 67
"3950" club, Mandalay Bay, 98
The Three Stooges (slot game), 67,
   93–94, 140
Throw the Dough (slot game), 69
Titanic, 61
Touring exhibits, 61–62
Tournaments. *See* Slot tournaments
Treasure Bay (Mississippi), 121–22
Treasure Island (Las Vegas), 101
Trebek, Alex, 65
Trivial Pursuit (slot game), 28
The Tropicana
   Atlantic City, 111
   Las Vegas, 99
Tropicana/West Tropicana Avenue
   (Las Vegas), 95, 99–100
Trump, Donald, 61, 71, 112,
   114–16
Trump Marina (Atlantic City), 115
Trump Plaza (Atlantic City), 106, 108,
   112–13, 122

Trump Taj Mahal (Atlantic City),
   114–15
Trump World's Fair Casino (Atlantic
   City), 112
TV cartoons (slot themes), 66–68
TV commercials (slot themes), 66
TV game shows (slot themes), 65,
   67–68
TV sitcoms (slot themes), 66–67

United States patent laws, 5
Universal, 13

Van Dyke, Jerry, 72
The Venetian (Las Vegas), 101–2
Video cartoon animation, 66
Video poker. *See* Poker games
Video slots. *See* Slot machines
   (1964–2004)
Virtual reels. *See* Telnaus virtual reel
   design
Voodoo Weasel, 115

Wales, Josey, 73
Watling, Tom, 6
Webster's Collegiate Dictionary, 1
West Flamingo (Las Vegas), 95
Westward Ho (Las Vegas), 102
Wheel of Fortune (slot game), 15, 65, 138
Wheel of Gold (slot game), 14
Whitman, Slim (guitar display), 95
The Who (guitar display), 95
Wicker Basket Capital of the World, 86
Wild Cherry (slot game), 118
WINNER, 27
WMS Gaming, 16, 28, 64, 66, 127
Wynn Las Vegas, 102
Wynn, Steve, 61, 100, 102, 111, 121, 138